A-Z® SOUTH E... ...NGL AND
Regiona... ...s

C000221538

CONTENTS

Key to Map Pages............ 2-3
Road Maps......................4-49
Index to Towns and Villages............50-61
Town Plans, Airport & Port Plans...62-72

REFERENCE

MOTORWAY	M2
Under Construction	
Proposed	
MOTORWAY JUNCTIONS WITH NUMBERS	
Unlimited interchange **4** Limited interchange **5**	
MOTORWAY SERVICE AREA	MEDWAY
with access from one carriageway only	Ⓢ
MAJOR ROAD SERVICE AREAS	PEASE POTTAGE
with 24 hour Facilities	Ⓢ
	61
PRIMARY ROUTE _ (with junction number)	A14
PRIMARY ROUTE DESTINATION	DOVER
DUAL CARRIAGEWAYS (A & B Roads)	A260
CLASS A ROAD	
CLASS B ROAD	B2011
MAJOR ROADS UNDER CONSTRUCTION	
MAJOR ROADS PROPOSED	
GRADIENT 1:5 (20%) & STEEPER (Ascent in direction of arrow)	≪
TOLL	TOLL
MILEAGE BETWEEN MARKERS	8
RAILWAY AND STATION	
LEVEL CROSSING AND TUNNEL	
RIVER OR CANAL	
COUNTY OR UNITARY AUTHORITY BOUNDARY	
NATIONAL BOUNDARY	+
BUILT-UP AREA	
VILLAGE OR HAMLET	○
WOODED AREA	
SPOT HEIGHT IN FEET	• 813
HEIGHT ABOVE SEA LEVEL 400' - 1,000' 122m - 305m	
1,000' - 1,400' 305m - 427m	
1,400' - 2,000' 427m - 610m	
2,000'+ 610m +	
NATIONAL GRID REFERENCE (Kilometres)	¹00
AREA COVERED BY TOWN PLAN	SEE PAGE 67

TOURIST INFORMATION

AIRPORT	✈
AIRFIELD	
HELIPORT	
BATTLE SITE AND DATE	⚔ 1066
CASTLE (Open to Public)	
CASTLE WITH GARDEN (Open to Public)	
CATHEDRAL, ABBEY, CHURCH, FRIARY, PRIORY	✝
COUNTRY PARK	
FERRY (Vehicular)	
(Foot only)	
GARDEN (Open to Public)	
GOLF COURSE ____ 9 HOLE ▶ 18 HOLE ____	▶18
HISTORIC BUILDING (Open to Public)	
HISTORIC BUILDING WITH GARDEN (Open to Public)	
HORSE RACECOURSE	
INFORMATION CENTRE	ℹ
LIGHTHOUSE	
MOTOR RACING CIRCUIT	
MUSEUM, ART GALLERY	
NATIONAL PARK OR FOREST PARK	
NATIONAL TRUST PROPERTY (Open)	NT
(Restricted Opening)	NT
NATURE RESERVE OR BIRD SANCTUARY	
NATURE TRAIL OR FOREST WALK	
PLACE OF INTEREST	Monument •
PICNIC SITE	
RAILWAY, STEAM OR NARROW GAUGE	
THEME PARK	
VIEWPOINT ____ 360 degrees	
180 degrees	
WILDLIFE PARK	
WINDMILL	
ZOO OR SAFARI PARK	

SCALE

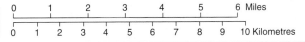

0   1   2   3   4   5   6 Miles
0   1   2   3   4   5   6   7   8   9   10 Kilometres

1:158,400
2.5 Miles to 1 Inch

Geographers' A-Z Map Company Ltd

Fairfield Road, Borough Green,
Sevenoaks, Kent TN15 8PP

01732 781000 (Enquiries & Trade Sales)
01732 783422 (Retail Sales)

Edition 9 2006
Copyright © Geographers' A-Z Map Company Ltd.

www.a-zmaps.co.uk

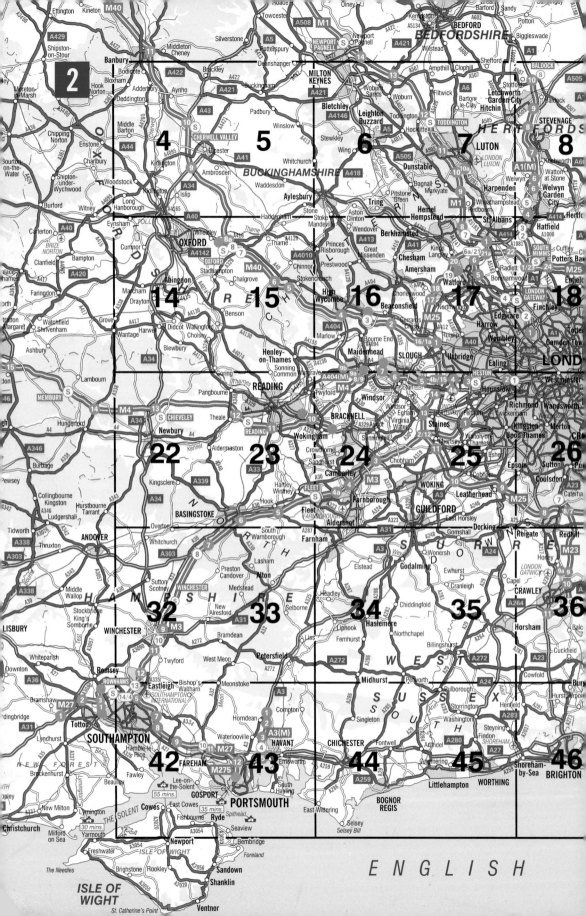

Grid squares: 9, 10, 11, 12, 13, 19, 20, 21, 27, 28, 29, 30, 31, 37, 38, 39, 40, 41, 47, 48, 49

IPSWICH · Woodbridge · Orford · Felixstowe · Harwich · Martlesham Heath · Kesgrave · Bawdsey · Chelmondiston · Thimley St. Mary · Shotley Gate · Parkeston · Holbrook · Bramford · Hadleigh · Capel St. Mary · Manningtree · Brantham · East Bergholt · Lawford · Ardleigh · Weeley · Thorpe-le-Soken · Kirby-le-Soken · Walton-on-the-Naze · Frinton-on-Sea · Clacton-on-Sea · St. Osyth · Brightlingsea · Wivenhoe · COLCHESTER · West Mersea · MERSEA ISLAND · Abberton Reservoir · Tiptree · Kelvedon · Coggeshall · Witham · Tollesbury · Maldon · Braintree · Halstead · Earls Colne · Gosfield · Sible Hedingham · Finchingfield · Great Bardfield · Thaxted · Great Dunmow · Lavenham · Monks Eleigh · Great Waldingfield · Long Melford · Sudbury · Clare · Cavendish · Haverhill · Kedington · Linton · Balsham · Saffron Walden · Steeple Bumpstead · Duxford · Sawston · Bishop's Stortford · Hatfield Heath · Birchanger Green · Nayland · West Bergholt

CHELMSFORD · Boreham · Writtle · Danbury · Bradwell-on-Sea · Southminster · Burnham-on-Crouch · Foulness Point · FOULNESS ISLAND · South Woodham Ferrers · Hockley · Rochford · Rayleigh · Wickford · SOUTHEND-ON-SEA · Great Wakering · Shoeburyness · BASILDON · Canvey Island · South Benfleet · BRENTWOOD · Ingatestone · Kelvedon Hatch · Chipping Ongar · North Weald Bassett · Epping · Harlow · Romford · Upminster · Dagenham · Hornchurch · THURROCK · Grays · Stanford-le-Hope · Tilbury · Cliffe · Grain · Gravesend · Strood · Dartford Crossing · Dartford · Swanley · Erith · Bexleyheath · Woolwich

Sheerness · ISLE OF SHEPPEY · Leysdown-on-Sea · Minster · Queenborough · Thamesport · The Swale · Sittingbourne · Faversham · Whitstable · HERNE BAY · MARGATE · Westgate on Sea · Birchington · NORTH FORELAND · BROADSTAIRS · RAMSGATE · Pegwell Bay · Sandwich · DEAL · Sarre · CANTERBURY · Sturry · Wingham · Eastry · Ash · ROCHESTER · GILLINGHAM · CHATHAM · MEDWAY · Snodland · Meopham · West Kingsdown · Sevenoaks · Westerham · Biggin Hill · Orpington · Swanley · MAIDSTONE · Hollingbourne · Bearsted · Lenham · Charing · Harrietsham · Chilham · Bridge · Barham · Elham · Lyminge · Whitfield · Kingsdown · SOUTH FORELAND · St. Margaret's at Cliffe · Temple Ewell · DOVER · STRAIT OF DOVER · Channel Tunnel · CHANNEL TUNNEL · FOLKESTONE · HYTHE · Dymchurch · New Romney · Littlestone-on-Sea · Greatstone-on-Sea · Lydd · ROMNEY MARSH · St. Mary's Bay · LONDON ASHFORD (Lydd) · ASHFORD · Wye · Pluckley · Headcorn · Bethersden · Biddenden · Hamstreet · Bonnington · DUNGENESS

TONBRIDGE · ROYAL TUNBRIDGE WELLS · Southborough · Penshurst · Leigh · Hildenborough · Paddock Wood · Pembury · Marden · Yalding · Staplehurst · Sutton Valence · Goudhurst · Cranbrook · Tenterden · Appledore · Rolvenden · Hawkhurst · Ticehurst · Wadhurst · Crowborough · Forest Row · Wych Cross · Uckfield · Heathfield · Burwash · Robertsbridge · Northiam · Broad Oak · Rye · Camber · Winchelsea · Rye Bay · Battle · Netherfield · Brede · Hastings · BEXHILL · Ninfield · Herstmonceux · Hailsham · Horam · East Hoathly · Lewes · Polegate · EASTBOURNE · East Dean · BEACHY HEAD · Seaford · Newhaven

CHANNEL · FRANCE · CAP GRIS-NEZ · BOULOGNE

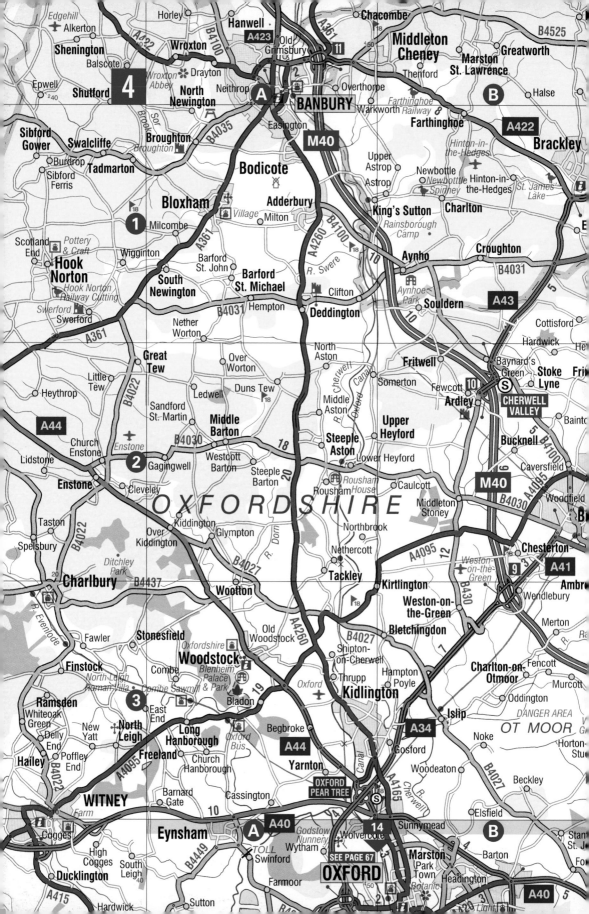

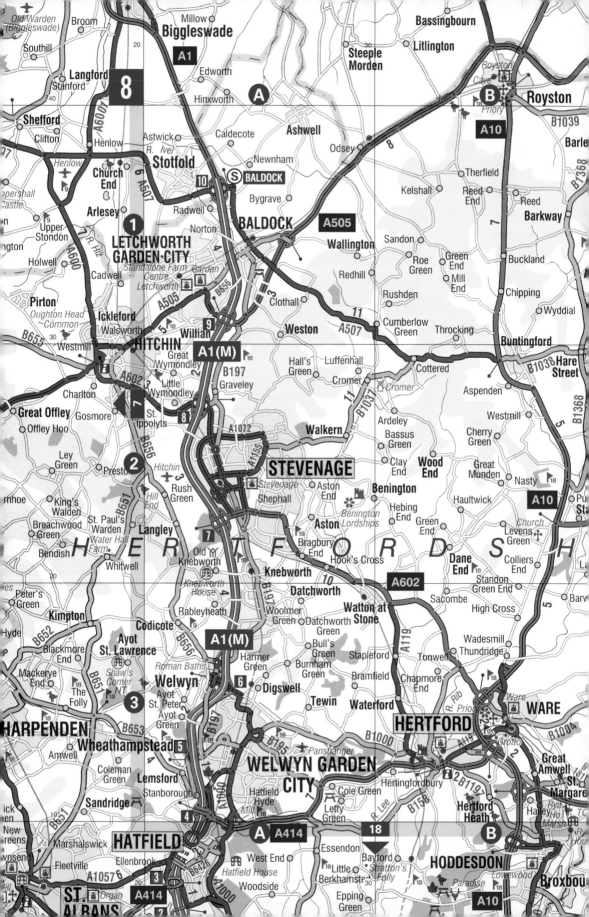

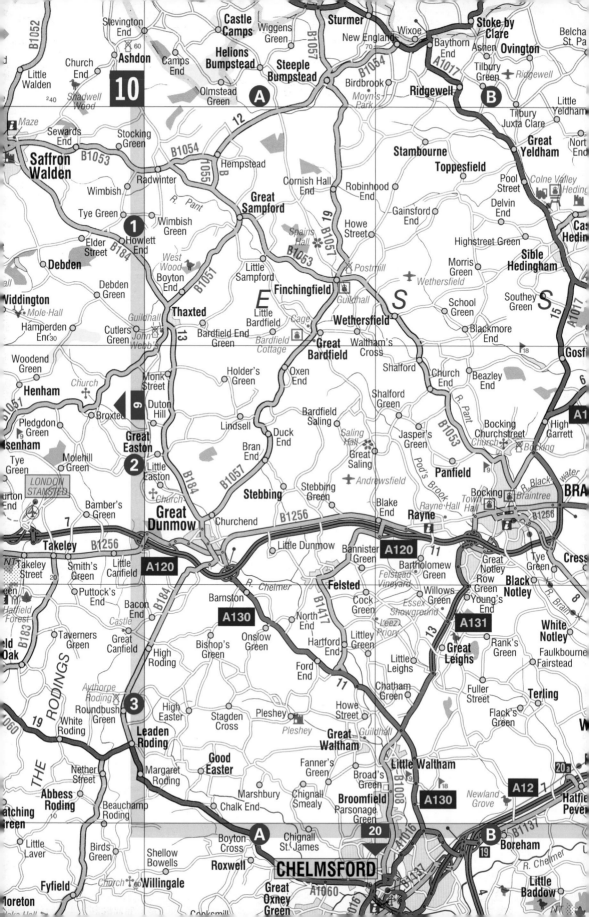

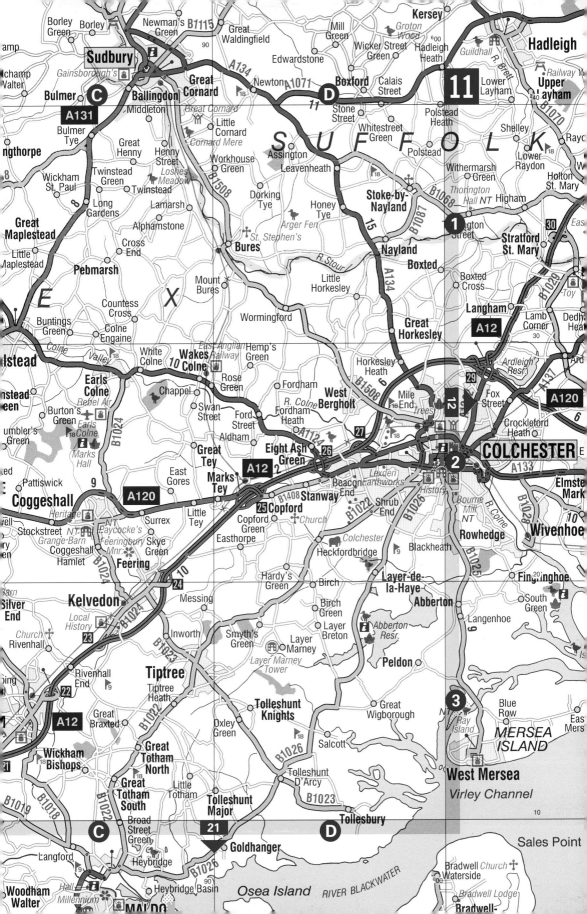

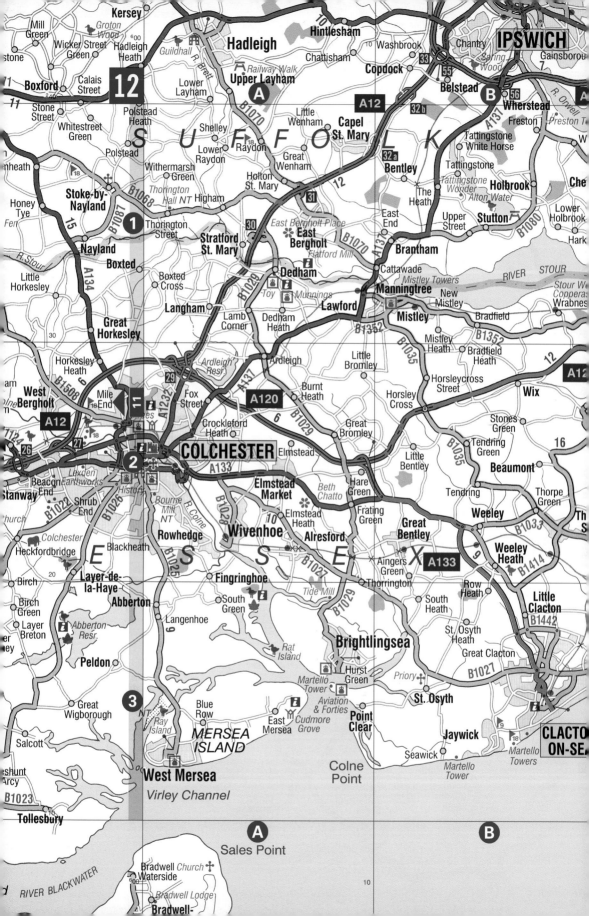

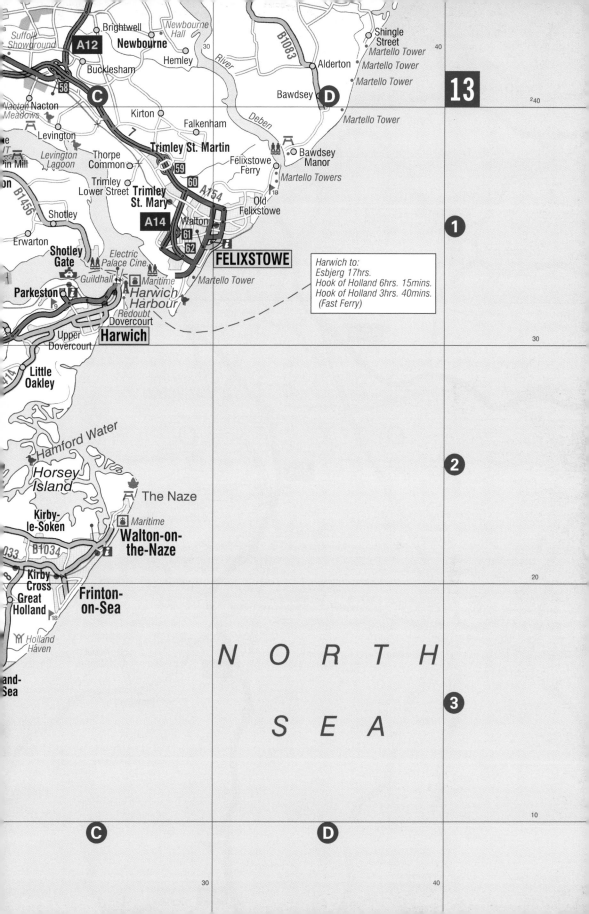

Suffolk
Showground

Brightwell
Newbourne
Hall
Shingle
Street

A12   Newbourne
Hemley
30
Alderton
Martello Tower
40

Buncklesham
River
Deben
Martello Tower

58
C
Nacton
Meadows
Kirton
Falkenham
B1083
Bawdsey
D
Martello Tower

13

240

Nacton
Levington
Thorpe
Common
Trimley St. Martin
7
Felixstowe
Ferry
Bawdsey
Manor

Levington
Lagoon
59
Martello Towers

Mill
Trimley
Lower Street
Trimley
St. Mary
60
A154
18
Old
Felixstowe

1

Shotley
A14
Walton

Erwarton
Shotley
Gate
Electric
Palace Cine.
61
62

Guildhall
Maritime
FELIXSTOWE

Parkeston
Harwich
Harbour
Martello Tower

Redoubt
Dovercourt

Harwich to:
Esbjerg 17hrs.
Hook of Holland 6hrs. 15mins.
Hook of Holland 3hrs. 40mins.
(Fast Ferry)

Upper
Dovercourt
Harwich

30

Little
Oakley

Hamford Water

Horsey
Island

The Naze

2

Kirby-
le-Soken
Maritime
Walton-on-
the-Naze

20

B1034

033
Kirby
Cross
Great
Holland
Frinton-
on-Sea
18

N O R T H

Holland
Haven

and-
Sea

S E A

3

10

C
D

30
40

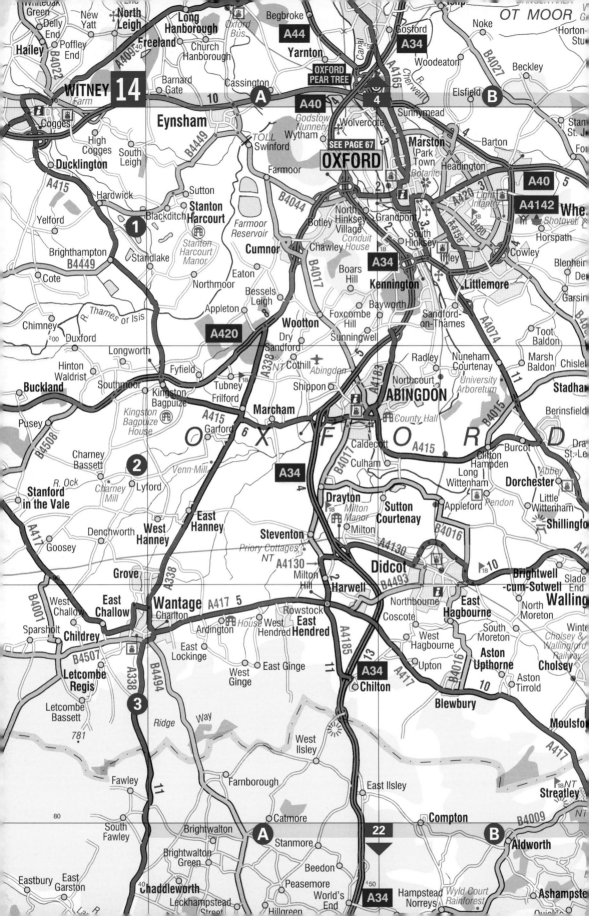

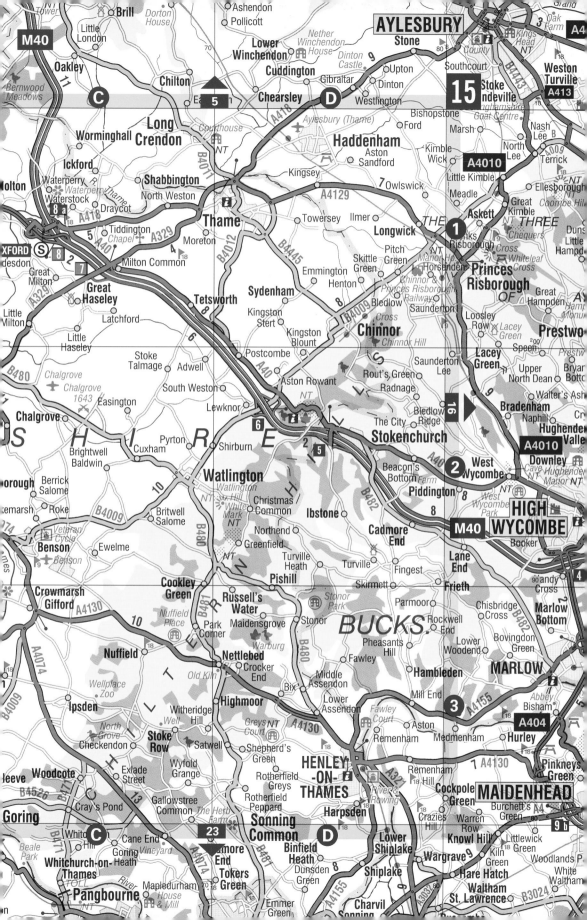

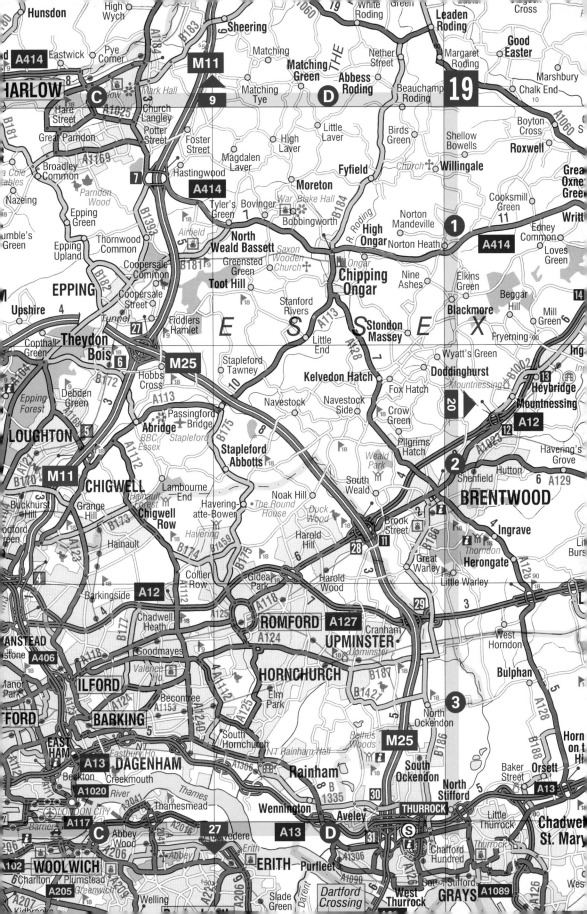

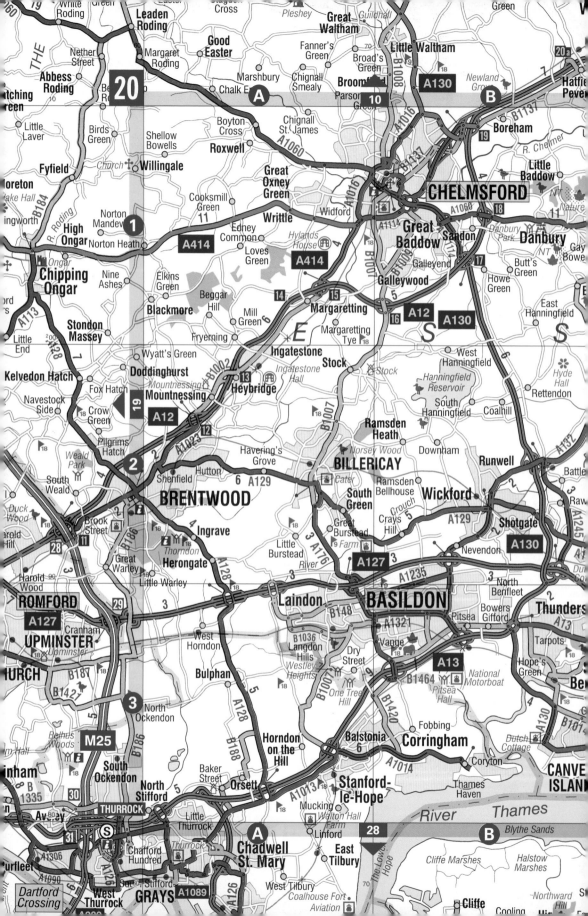

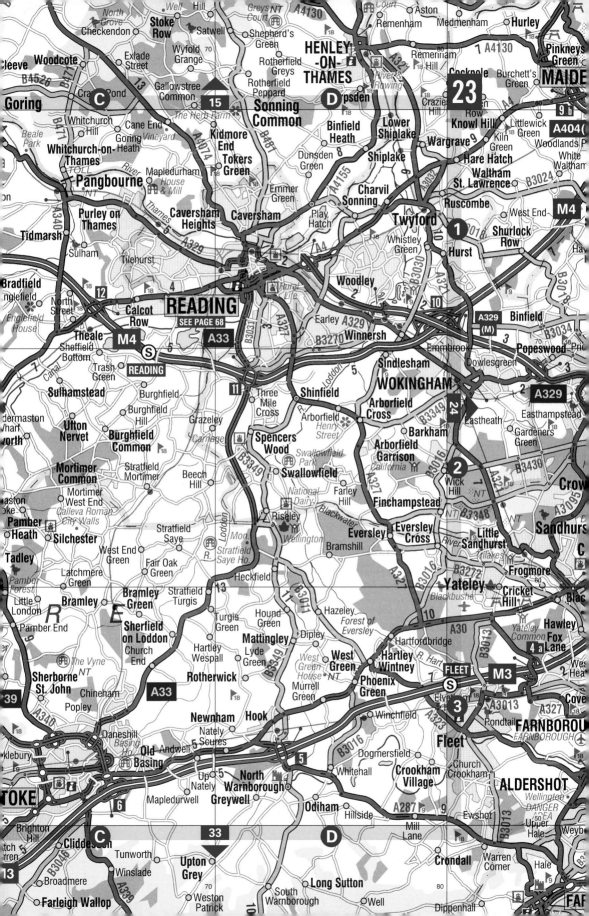

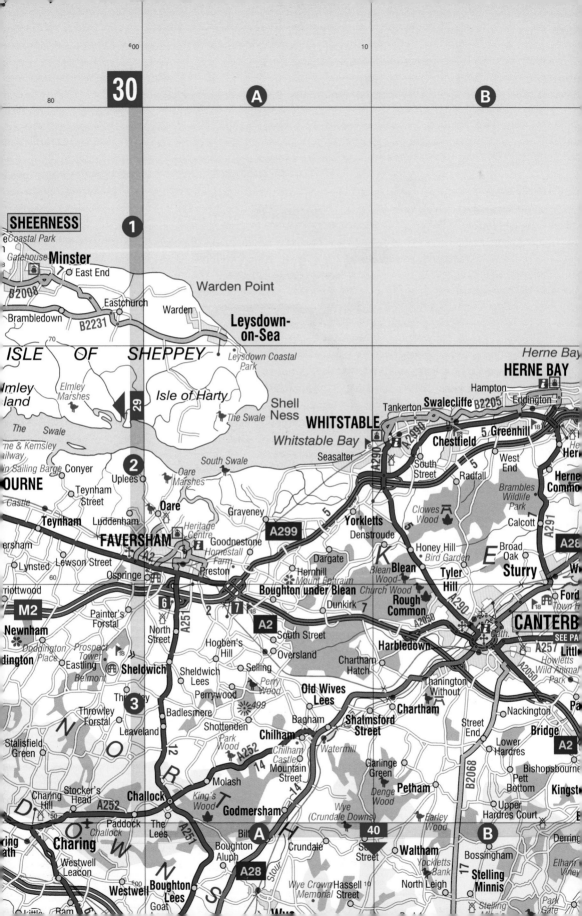

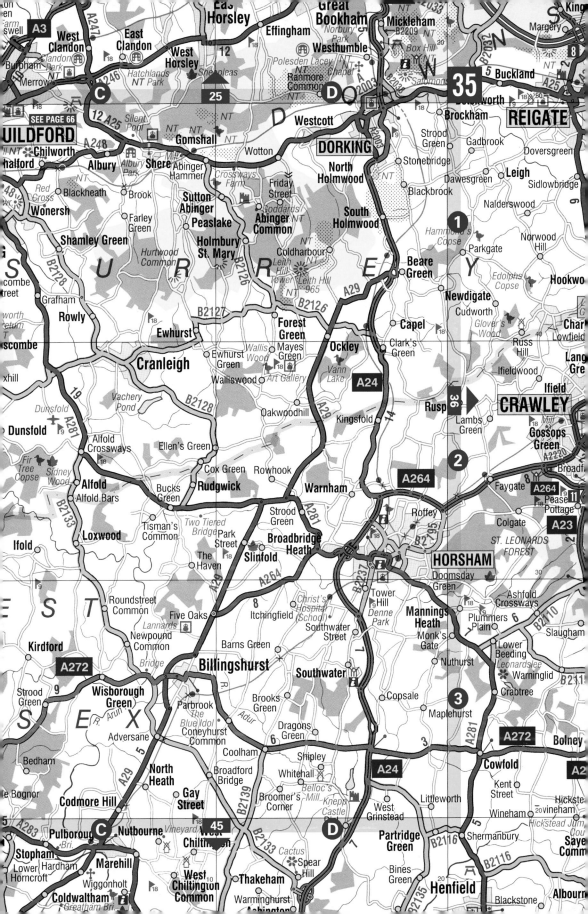

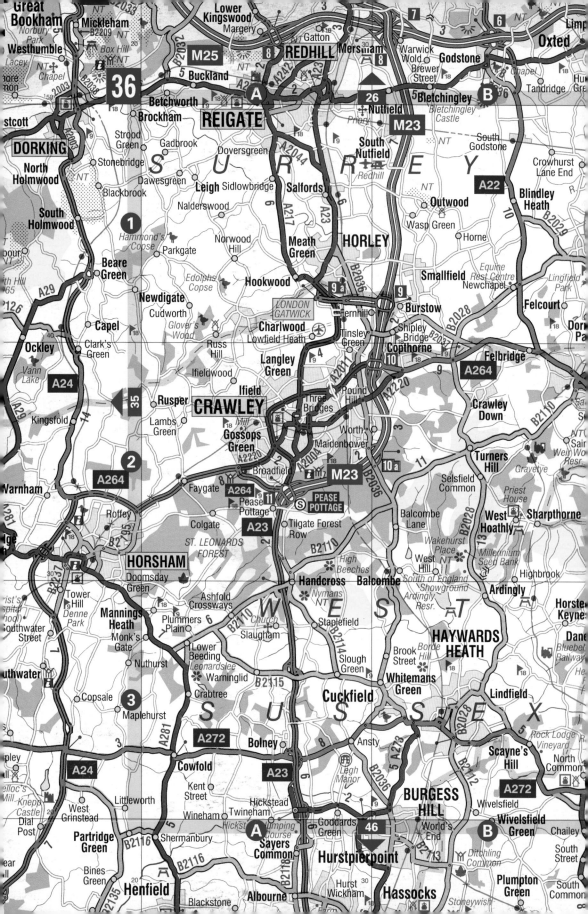

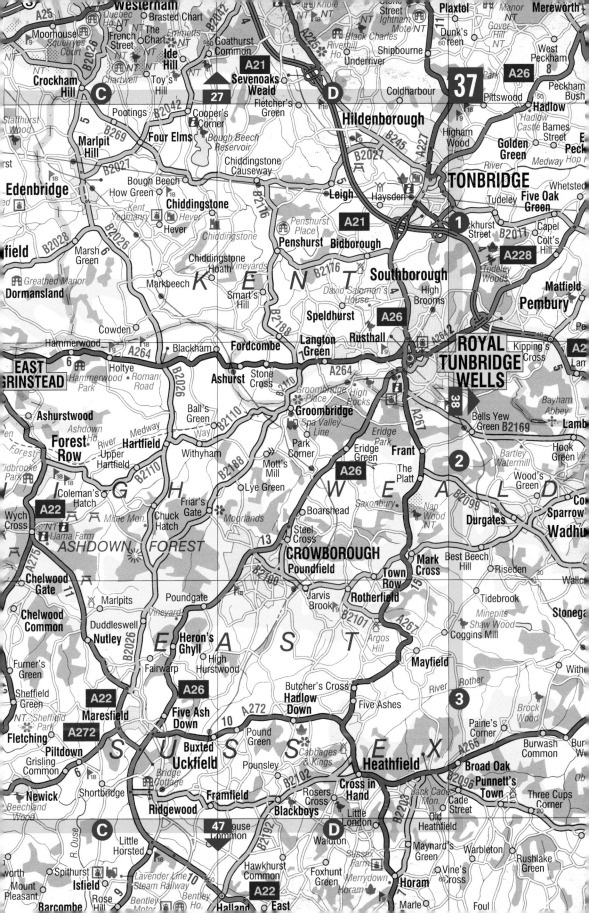

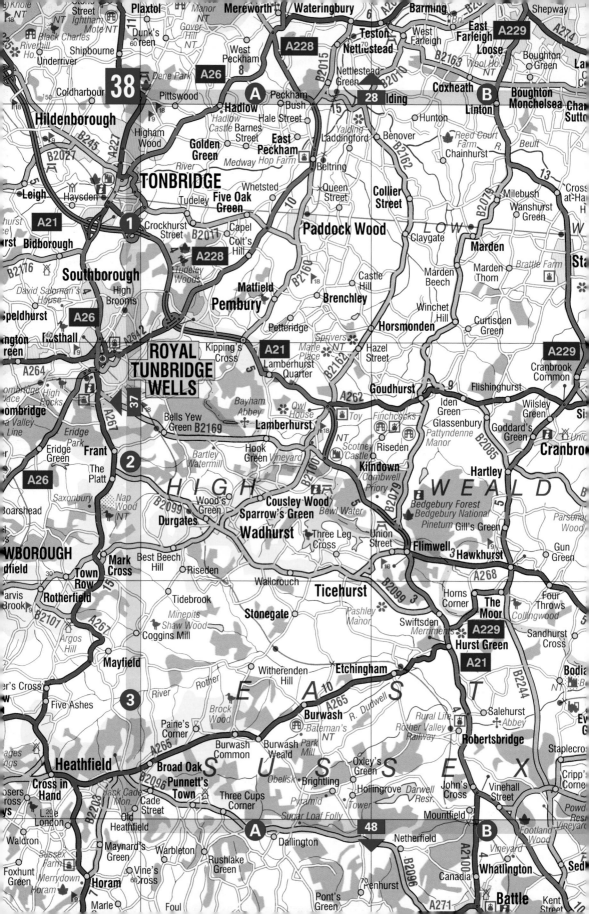

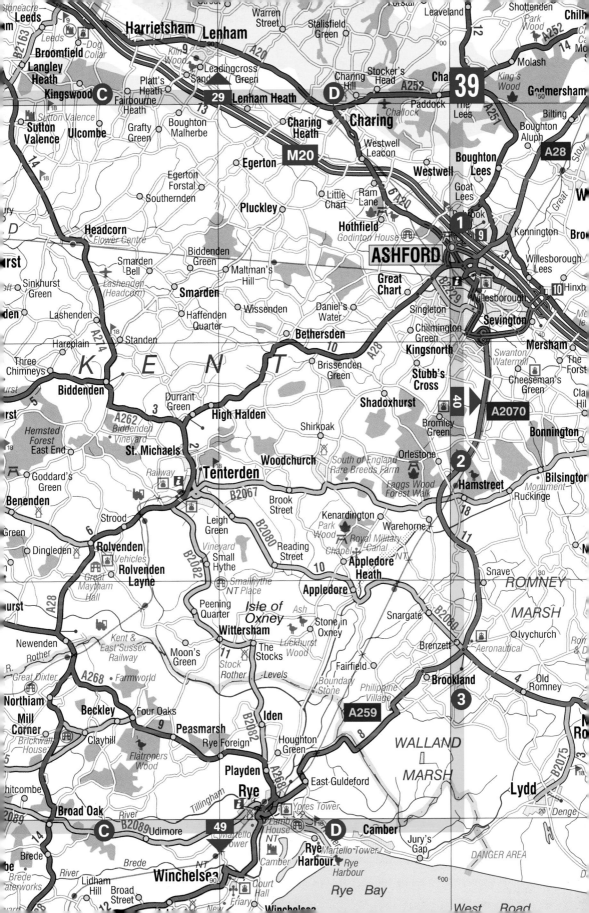

Adisham

Heronden

Chillenden
Knowlton

Finglesham
Betteshanger

Local
History

Victoriana
Time-Ball
Tower

DEAL
Deal

*The
Downs*

41

Nonington

Knowlton

Northbourne

*Northbourne
Court*

Sholden

**Great
Monge
Ripple**

C **31**

Womens

Frogham

Tilmanston

Elvington

*East Kent
Railway*

D

Walmer

Walmer

¹50

Wools
Village

Bartrestone

East
Studdal

Sutton

Eythorne

**Shepherdswell
or Sibertswold**

Coldred

Ashley

Ringwould

West
Langdon

Kingsdown

Woolage
Green

NT

NT

*DANGER
AREA*

A256

Whitfield

Wootton

Lydden

Lydden

Temple Ewell

Ewell
Minnis

Kearsney

West
Langdon

Martin

East
Langdon

Martin Mill

*Dover Patrol
Monument*

**St. Margaret's
at Cliffe** **1**

*St. John's
Commandery*

River

Guston

NT

The Bay

A256

A2

Buckland

West
Cliffe

NT

St. Margaret's Bay

The Pines

*Butterfly
Centre*

*Crabble
Corn Mill*

*St. Radigund's
Abbey*

NT

SOUTH FORELAND

Alkham

SEE PAGE 63
DOVER

40

Drellingore

Maxton

West
Hougham

Church
Hougham

Hawkinge

**Capel-le-
Ferne**

*Western
Docks*

A20

Dover to:
Boulogne 50mins. (Fast Ferry)
Calais 1hr. 10mins.
Dunkirk 2hrs.

*Samphire
Hoe*

**East Wear
Bay**

CHANNEL TUNNEL
Folkestone to
Calais 35mins.

*Martello
Towers*

2

FOLKESTONE

SEE PAGE 68

STRAIT OF DOVER

30

3

E N G L I S H

C H A N N E L

C

D

30

40

20

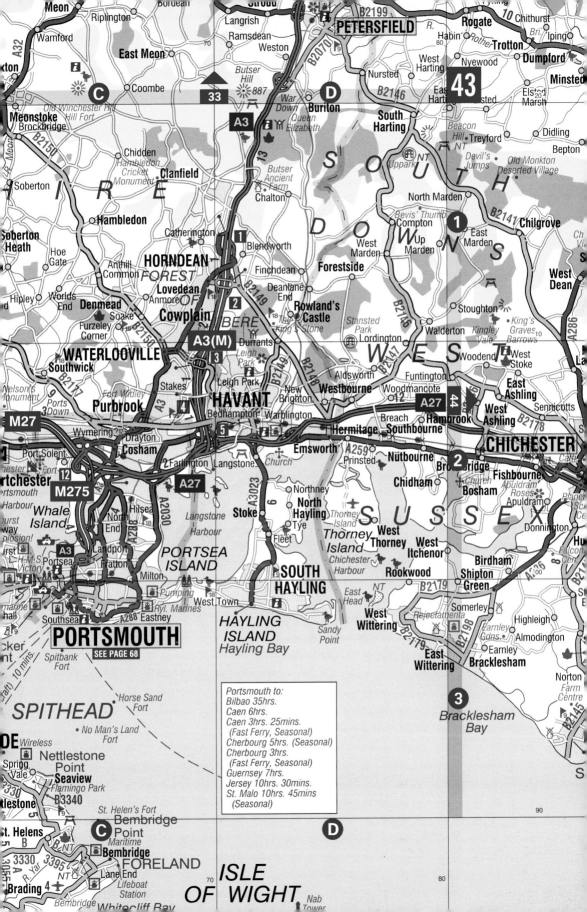

Map — Portsmouth / Chichester / Hayling Island area

Top row:
Meon · Bordean · Stroud · B2199 · Rogate · Chithurst
Riplington · Langrish · **PETERSFIELD** · Habin · Trotton · Bri. Iping
Warnford · Ramsdean · Weston · B2070 · West Harting · Nyewood · **Dumpford**
East Meon · Coombe · Nursted · Minsted · Elsted Marsh

A32 · A3 · B2146 · East Harting · **43**

C · Butser Hill · 887 · War Down · Queen Elizabeth · **Buriton** · **D** · South Harting · Beacon Hill · Treyford · Didling
Meonstoke · Brockbridge · Old Winchester Hill Hill Fort · **33** · Uppark NT · Devil's Jumps · Old Monkton Deserted Village · Bepton

B2150 · Chidden · Hambledon Cricket Monument · **Clanfield** · Butser Ancient Farm · Chalton · North Marden · Bevis' Thumb · Compton · B2141 · Up Marden · East Marden · **Chilgrove** · **1**

Soberton · **Hambledon** · Catherington · **1** · Blendworth · Finchdean · **Forestside** · West Marden · Up Marden · Stoughton · King's Graves Barrows · **West Dean** · A286

Soberton Heath · Hoe Gate · **HORNDEAN** · B2149 · Deanlane End · **Rowland's Castle** · King's Stone · Stansted Park · Lordington · Walderton · Kingley Vale · Woodend · West Stoke · La

Hipley · Worlds End · **Denmead** · Anthill Common · Anmore · **Lovedean** · **2** · 18 · Leigh Park · Durrants · WEST SUSSEX · B2147 · Funtington · **East Ashling** · Sennicotts

WATERLOOVILLE · Southwick · **A3(M)** · **3** · Leigh Park · Stakes · **HAVANT** · New Brighton · Aldsworth · **Westbourne** · Woodmancote · 12 · **A27** · **44** · West Ashling · B2178

M27 · Fort Widley · **Purbrook** · Ports Down · A3 · **4** · Bedhampton · Warblington · Breach · **Hambrook** · **Southbourne** · West Ashling · **CHICHESTER**

Nelson's Monument · B2177 · Drayton · **5** · **Hermitage** · Southbourne · **2** · Broad Bridge · Fishbourne
M275 · 12 · Wymering · **Cosham** · Farlington · Langstone · Emsworth · A259 · Prinsted · **Nutbourne** · **Bosham** · Apuldram Roses · Apuldram
rtchester · Port Solent · Portsmouth Harbour · Church · Northney · **Chidham** · Church · Donnington

A3 · Norm End · Hilsea · Langstone Harbour · **North Hayling** · Tye · **West Thorney** · **West Itchenor** · **Birdham**
Whale Island · Landport · Fratton · **Stoke** · Thorney Island · Chichester Harbour · **Rookwood** · **Shipton Green** · A286

H.M.S. Victory · Portsea · Milton · **PORTSEA ISLAND** · Fleet · **West Thorney** · B2179 · **Somerley** · Highleigh · Almodington
marine hall · Southsea · A288 · Eastney · West Town · Ryl. Marines · **East Head** NT · **West Wittering** · Earnley Gdns · **Earnley**

PORTSMOUTH SEE PAGE 68 · **HAYLING ISLAND** Hayling Bay · Sandy Point · B2179 · **East Wittering** · **Bracklesham** · Norton Farm Centre · B2145

SPITHEAD · Spitbank Fort · Horse Sand Fort · **SOUTH HAYLING** · **3** · **Bracklesham Bay** · 90

craft · 10 mins · No Man's Land Fort

DE · Wireless · **Nettlestone Point** · Spring Vale · **Seaview** · Flamingo Park · B3340

St. Helen's Fort · **Bembridge Point** · Maritime · **C** · **D**
St. Helens · **Bembridge** · **FORELAND** NT · Lane End · **ISLE OF WIGHT** · 80
Brading · Bembridge · R. Yar · Lifeboat Station · Nab Tower · Whitecliff Bay · 70

Portsmouth to:
Bilbao 35hrs.
Caen 6hrs.
Caen 3hrs. 25mins.
(Fast Ferry, Seasonal)
Cherbourg 5hrs. (Seasonal)
Cherbourg 3hrs.
(Fast Ferry, Seasonal)
Guernsey 7hrs.
Jersey 10hrs. 30mins.
St. Malo 10hrs. 45mins.
(Seasonal)

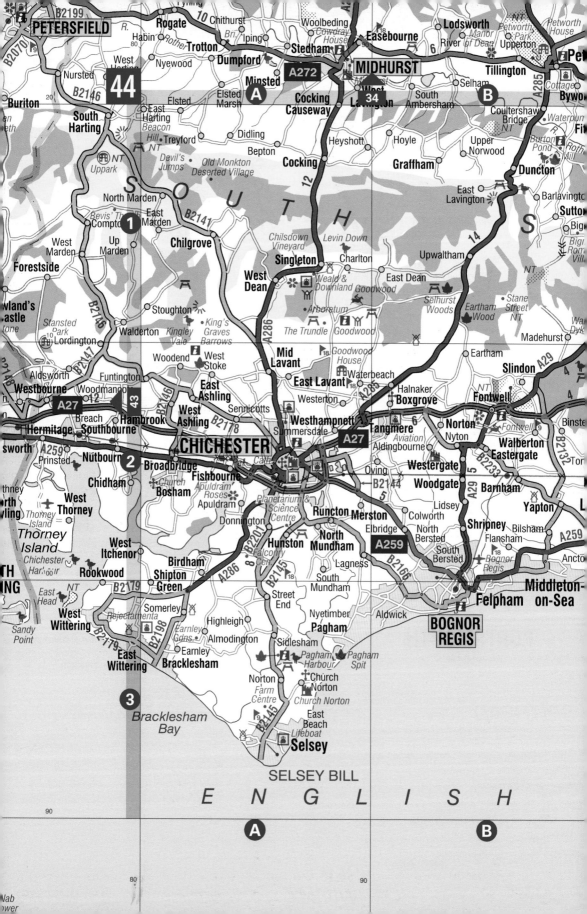

Mill
Corner
Brickwall
House
Clayhill
Peasmarsh
Rye Foreign
Iden
B2082
Houghton
Green
WALLAND

Flatropers
Wood
Playden
A259
East Guldeford
MARSH
Lydd
B2075

C
River
Rye
39
Ypres To
D
49
Denge
Marsh

Udimore
Martello
Tower
Lamb
House
NT
Camber
Jury's
Gap

S E X
Broad
Oak
B2089
Brede
Camber
Rye
Harbour
Martello Tower
Rye
Harbour
DANGER AREA

Brede
River
Winchelsea
NT
Camber

Brede
erworks
Lidham
Hill
Broad
Street
Court
Hall
Rye Bay
West Road

Westfield
Icklesham
New
Gate
Friary
Winchelsea
Beach
1

Three Oaks
Guestling
Thorn
10

A28
Guestling
Green
Pett
Guestling
Wood
Cliff End

ldslow
B2093
A259
Fairlight
Cove
2

St.
elen's
Ore
Fairlight
Hastings

B2701
Daves
100

HASTINGS
Shipwreck Centre &
Underwater World

E N G L I S H

C H A N N E L

3

90

C
D

90
600

INDEX TO CITIES, TOWNS, VILLAGES, HAMLETS & LOCATIONS

(1) A strict alphabetical order is used e.g. Abbotstone follows Abbots Langley but precedes Abbots Worthy.

(2) The map reference given refers to the actual map square in which the town spot or built-up area is located and not to the place name.

(3) Only one reference is given although due to page overlaps the place may appear on more than one page.

(4) Where two places of the same name occur in the same County or Unitary Authority, the nearest large town is also given;
e.g. Ash. *Kent* . . . .3C **31** (Sandwich) indicates that Ash is located in square 3C on page **31** and is situated near Sandwich in the County of Kent.

(5) Major towns are shown in bold i.e. **Brighton.** *Brig* . . . .2B **46** & **62.** Where they appear on a Town Plan a second page reference is given.

COUNTIES AND UNITARY AUTHORITIES with the abbreviations used in this index

Bedfordshire : *Beds*
Bracknell Forest : *Brac*
Brighton & Hove : *Brig*
Buckinghamshire : *Buck*
Cambridgeshire : *Cambs*
East Sussex : *E Sus*
Essex : *Essx*
Greater London : *G Lon*

Hampshire : *Hants*
Hertfordshire : *Herts*
Isle of Wight : *IOW*
Kent : *Kent*
Luton : *Lutn*
Medway : *Medw*
Milton Keynes : *Mil*
Northamptonshire : *Nptn*

Oxfordshire : *Oxon*
Portsmouth : *Port*
Reading : *Read*
Slough : *Slo*
Southampton : *Sotn*
Southend-on-Sea : *S'end*
Suffolk : *Suff*
Surrey : *Surr*

Thurrock : *Thur*
West Berkshire : *W Ber*
West Sussex : *W Sus*
Windsor & Maidenhead : *Wind*
Wokingham : *Wok*

A

Abberton. *Essx* 3A **12**
Abbess Roding. *Essx* 3D **9**
Abbey Wood. *G Lon* 1C **27**
Abbots Langley. *Herts* 1C **17**
Abbotstone. *Hants* 2B **32**
Abbots Worthy. *Hants* 2A **32**
Abingdon. *Oxon* 2A **14**
Abinger Common. *Surr* 1D **35**
Abinger Hammer. *Surr* 1C **35**
Abridge. *Essx* 2C **19**
Acol. *Kent* 2D **31**
Acrise. *Kent* 1B **40**
Acton. *G Lon* 3D **17**
Adderbury. *Oxon* 1A **4**
Addington. *Buck* 2D **5**
Addington. *G Lon* 2B **26**
Addington. *Kent* 3A **28**
Addiscombe. *G Lon* 2B **26**
Addlestone. *Surr* 2C **25**
Adgestone. *IOW* 3B **42**
Adisham. *Kent* 3C **31**
Adstock. *Buck* 1D **5**
Adversane. *W Sus* 3C **35**
Adwell. *Oxon* 2C **15**
Aingers Green. *Essx* 2B **12**
Akeley. *Buck* 1D **5**
Albourne. *W Sus* 1A **46**
Albury. *Herts* 2C **9**
Albury. *Surr* 1C **35**
Alciston. *E Sus* 2D **47**
Aldbury. *Herts* 3B **6**
Aldenham. *Herts* 2D **17**
Aldermaston. *W Ber* 2B **22**
Aldermaston Stoke. *W Ber* 2C **23**
Aldermaston Wharf. *W Ber* 2C **23**
Aldershot. *Hants* 3A **24**
Alderton. *Suff* 1D **13**
Aldham. *Essx* 2D **11**
Aldingbourne. *W Sus* 2B **44**
Aldington. *Kent* 2A **40**
Aldsworth. *W Sus* 2D **43**
Aldwick. *W Sus* 3B **44**
Aldworth. *W Ber* 1B **22**
Aley Green. *Beds* 3C **7**
Alfold. *Surr* 2C **35**
Alfold Bars. *W Sus* 2C **35**
Alfold Crossways. *Surr* 2C **35**
Alfriston. *E Sus* 2D **47**
Alkerton. *Oxon* 1A **4**
Alkham. *Kent* 1C **41**
Allbrook. *Hants* 3A **32**
Allen's Green. *Herts* 3C **9**
Allhallows. *Medw* 1C **29**
Allhallows-on-Sea. *Medw* 1C **29**
Allington. *Kent* 3B **28**
Almodington. *W Sus* 3A **44**
Alphamstone. *Essx* 1C **11**
Alresford. *Essx* 2A **12**
Althorne. *Essx* 2D **21**
Alton. *Hants* 2D **33**
Alverstoke. *Hants* 3B **42**
Amberley. *W Sus* 1C **45**
Ambrosden. *Oxon* 3C **5**
Amersham. *Buck* 2B **16**
Ampfield. *Hants* 3A **32**
Ampthill. *Beds* 1C **7**
Amwell. *Herts* 3D **7**
Ancton. *W Sus* 2B **44**
Andover. *Hants* 1A **32**
Andover Down. *Hants* 1A **32**
Andwell. *Hants* 3C **23**
Angmering. *W Sus* 2C **45**
Angmering-on-Sea. *W Sus* 2C **45**
Anmore. *Hants* 1C **43**

Ansteadbrook. *Surr* 2B **34**
Anstey. *Herts* 1C **9**
Ansty. *W Sus* 3A **36**
Anthill Common. *Hants* 1C **43**
Appledore. *Kent* 3D **39**
Appledore Heath. *Kent* 2D **39**
Appleford. *Oxon* 2B **14**
Applemore. *Hants* 2A **42**
Appleton. *Oxon* 1A **14**
Apsley End. *Beds* 1D **7**
Apuldram. *W Sus* 2A **44**
Arborfield. *Wok* 2D **23**
Arborfield Cross. *Wok* 2D **23**
Arborfield Garrison. *Wok* 2D **23**
Ardeley. *Herts* 2B **8**
Ardingly. *W Sus* 3B **36**
Ardington. *Oxon* 3A **14**
Ardleigh. *Essx* 2A **12**
Ardley. *Oxon* 2B **4**
Arford. *Hants* 2A **34**
Arkesden. *Essx* 1C **9**
Arkley. *G Lon* 2A **18**
Arlesey. *Beds* 1D **7**
Arlington. *E Sus* 2D **47**
Arreton. *IOW* 3B **42**
Arundel. *W Sus* 2C **45**
Ascot. *Wind* 2B **24**
Ash. *Kent* 3C **31**
. . . . (nr. Sandwich)
Ash. *Kent* 2A **28**
. . . . (nr. Swanley)
Ash. *Surr* 3A **24**
Ashampstead. *W Ber* 1B **22**
Ashdon. *Essx* 1D **9**
Ashe. *Hants* 3B **22**
Asheldham. *Essx* 1D **21**
Ashen. *Essx* 1B **10**
Ashendon. *Buck* 3D **5**
Ashey. *IOW* 3B **42**
Ashfield. *Hants* 1A **42**
Ashfold Crossways. *W Sus* 3A **36**
Ashford. *Kent* 1A **40**
Ashford. *Surr* 1C **25**
Ashford Hill. *Hants* 2B **22**
Ashingdon. *Essx* 2C **21**
Ashington. *W Sus* 1D **45**
Ashlett. *Hants* 2A **42**
Ashley. *Hants* 2A **32**
Ashley. *Kent* 1D **41**
Ashley Green. *Buck* 1B **16**
Ashmansworth. *Hants* 3A **22**
Ashmore Green. *W Ber* 2B **22**
Ashtead. *Surr* 3D **25**
Ashurst. *Kent* 2D **37**
Ashurst. *W Sus* 1D **45**
Ashurstwood. *W Sus* 2C **37**
Ash Vale. *Surr* 3A **24**
Ashwell. *Herts* 1A **8**
Askett. *Buck* 1A **16**
Aspenden. *Herts* 2B **8**
Aspley Guise. *Beds* 1B **6**
Aspley Heath. *Beds* 1B **6**
Assington. *Suff* 1D **11**
Aston. *Herts* 2A **8**
Aston. *Wok* 3D **15**
Aston Abbotts. *Buck* 3A **6**
Aston Clinton. *Buck* 3A **6**
Aston End. *Herts* 2A **8**
Aston Rowant. *Oxon* 2D **15**
Aston Sandford. *Buck* 1D **15**
Aston Tirrold. *Oxon* 3B **14**
Aston Upthorpe. *Oxon* 3B **14**
Astrop. *Nptn* 1B **4**
Astwick. *Beds* 1A **8**
Astwood. *W Sus* 2C **45**
Audley End. *Essx* 1D **9**
Aveley. *Thur* 3D **19**

Avington. *Hants* 2B **32**
Axford. *Hants* 1C **33**
Aylesbury. *Buck* 3A **6**
Aylesford. *Kent* 3B **28**
Aylesham. *Kent* 3C **31**
Aynho. *Nptn* 1B **4**
Ayot Green. *Herts* 3A **8**
Ayot St Lawrence. *Herts* 3D **7**
Ayot St Peter. *Herts* 3A **8**

B

Babb's Green. *Herts* 3B **8**
Bacon End. *Essx* 3A **10**
Badgers Mount. *Kent* 2C **27**
Badlesmere. *Kent* 3A **30**
Badshot Lea. *Surr* 1A **34**
Bagham. *Kent* 3A **30**
Bagnor. *W Ber* 2A **22**
Bagshot. *Surr* 2B **24**
Bailey Green. *Hants* 3C **33**
Bainton. *Oxon* 2B **4**
Baker Street. *Thur* 3A **20**
Balcombe. *W Sus* 2B **36**
Balcombe Lane. *W Sus* 2B **36**
Baldock. *Herts* 1A **8**
Baldslow. *E Sus* 1C **49**
Ballards Gore. *Essx* 2D **21**
Ball Hill. *Hants* 2A **22**
Ballingdon. *Suff* 1C **11**
Ballinger Common. *Buck* 1B **16**
Balls Cross. *W Sus* 3B **34**
Ball's Green. *E Sus* 2C **37**
Balscote. *Oxon* 1A **4**
Balstonia. *Thur* 3A **20**
Bamber's Green. *Essx* 2D **9**
Banbury. *Oxon* 1A **4**
Bannister Green. *Essx* 2A **10**
Banstead. *Surr* 3A **26**
Bapchild. *Kent* 2D **29**
Barcombe. *E Sus* 1C **47**
Barcombe Cross. *E Sus* 1C **47**
Bardfield End Green. *Essx* 1A **10**
Bardfield Saling. *Essx* 2A **10**
Barford. *Hants* 2A **34**
Barford St John. *Oxon* 1A **4**
Barford St Michael. *Oxon* 1A **4**
Barfrestone. *Kent* 3C **31**
Barham. *Kent* 3C **31**
Barkham. *Wok* 2D **23**
Barking. *G Lon* 3C **19**
Barkingside. *G Lon* 3C **19**
Barkway. *Herts* 1B **8**
Barlavington. *W Sus* 1B **44**
Barley. *Herts* 1B **8**
Barling. *Essx* 3D **21**
Barming. *Kent* 3B **28**
Barming Heath. *Kent* 3B **28**
Barnard Gate. *Oxon* 3A **4**
Barnes. *G Lon* 1A **26**
Barnes Street. *Kent* 1A **38**
Barnet. *G Lon* 2A **18**
Barnham. *W Sus* 2B **44**
Barns Green. *W Sus* 3D **35**
Barnston. *Essx* 3A **10**
Bartholomew Green. *Essx* 2B **10**
Barton. *IOW* 3B **42**
Barton. *Oxon* 1B **14**
Barton Hartsthorn. *Buck* 1C **5**
Barton-le-Clay. *Beds* 1C **7**
Barton Stacey. *Hants* 1A **32**
Barwick. *Herts* 3B **8**
Basildon. *Essx* 3B **20**
Basingstoke. *Hants* 3C **23**
Bassett. *Sotn* 1A **42**
Bassingbourn. *Cambs* 1B **8**

Bassus Green. *Herts* 2B **8**
Batchworth. *Herts* 2C **17**
Battersea. *G Lon* 1A **26**
Battle. *E Sus* 1B **48**
Battlesbridge. *Essx* 2B **20**
Battlesden. *Beds* 2B **6**
Batt's Corner. *Surr* 1A **34**
Baughurst. *Hants* 2B **22**
Bawdsey. *Suff* 1D **13**
Bawdsey Manor. *Suff* 1D **13**
Baybridge. *Hants* 3B **32**
Bayford. *Herts* 1B **18**
Baynard's Green. *Oxon* 2B **4**
Baythorn End. *Essx* 1B **10**
Bayworth. *Oxon* 1B **14**
Beachampton. *Buck* 1D **5**
Beacon End. *Essx* 2D **11**
Beacon Hill. *Surr* 2A **34**
Beacon's Bottom. *Buck* 2D **15**
Beaconsfield. *Buck* 2B **16**
Beacontree. *G Lon* 3C **19**
Beamond End. *Buck* 2B **16**
Bean. *Kent* 1D **27**
Beanshanger. *Nptn* 1D **5**
Beare Green. *Surr* 1D **35**
Bearsted. *Kent* 3B **28**
Beauchamp Roding. *Essx* 3D **9**
Beaulieu. *Hants* 2A **42**
Beaumont. *Essx* 2B **12**
Beauworth. *Hants* 3B **32**
Beazley End. *Essx* 2B **10**
Beckenham. *G Lon* 2B **26**
Beckley. *E Sus* 3C **39**
Beckley. *Oxon* 3B **4**
Beckton. *G Lon* 3C **19**
Becontree. *G Lon* 3C **19**
Beddingham. *E Sus* 2C **47**
Beddington. *G Lon* 2A **26**
Bedham. *W Sus* 3C **35**
Bedhampton. *Hants* 2D **43**
Bedlar's Green. *Essx* 3D **9**
Bedmond. *Herts* 1C **17**
Beech. *Hants* 2C **33**
Beech Hill. *W Ber* 2C **23**
Beedon. *W Ber* 1A **22**
Beenham. *W Ber* 2B **22**
Begbroke. *Oxon* 3A **4**
Beggar Hill. *Essx* 1A **20**
Bekesbourne. *Kent* 3B **30**
Belchamp Otten. *Essx* 1C **11**
Belchamp St Paul. *Essx* 1B **10**
Belchamp Walter. *Essx* 1C **11**
Bellingdon. *Buck* 1B **16**
Bells Yew Green. *E Sus* 2A **38**
Belsize. *Herts* 1C **17**
Belstead. *Suff* 1B **12**
Beltinge. *Kent* 2B **30**
Beltring. *Kent* 1A **38**
Belvedere. *G Lon* 1C **27**
Bembridge. *IOW* 3C **43**
Bendish. *Herts* 2D **7**
Benenden. *Kent* 2C **39**
Benington. *Herts* 2A **8**
Benover. *Kent* 1B **38**
Benson. *Oxon* 2C **15**
Bentley. *Hants* 1D **33**
Bentley. *Suff* 1B **12**
Bentley Heath. *Herts* 2A **18**
Bentworth. *Hants* 1C **33**
Bepton. *W Sus* 1A **44**
Berden. *Essx* 2C **9**
Berinsfield. *Oxon* 2B **14**
Berkhamsted. *Herts* 1B **16**
Bermondsey. *G Lon* 1B **26**
Berrick Salome. *Oxon* 2C **15**
Berry's Green. *G Lon* 3C **27**
Berwick. *E Sus* 2D **47**

Bessels Leigh. *Oxon* 1A **14**
Best Beech Hill. *E Sus* 2A **38**
Betchworth. *Surr* 3A **26**
Bethersden. *Kent* 1D **39**
Bethnal Green. *G Lon* 3B **18**
Betsham. *Kent* 1A **28**
Betteshanger. *Kent* 3D **31**
Bevendean. *Brig* 2B **46**
Bexhill. *E Sus* 2B **48**
Bexley. *G Lon* 1C **27**
Bexleyheath. *G Lon* 1C **27**
Bexleyhill. *W Sus* 3B **34**
Bicester. *Oxon* 2B **4**
Bicknacre. *Essx* 1B **20**
Bicknor. *Kent* 3C **29**
Bidborough. *Kent* 1D **37**
Biddenden. *Kent* 2C **39**
Biddenden Green. *Kent* 1C **39**
Biddlesden. *Buck* 1C **5**
Bierton. *Buck* 3A **6**
Biggin Hill. *G Lon* 3C **27**
Biggin Hill (London) Airport.
    G Lon 2C **27**
Biggleswade. *Beds* 1A **8**
Bighton. *Hants* 2C **33**
Bignor. *W Sus* 1B **44**
Billericay. *Essx* 2A **20**
Billingshurst. *W Sus* 3C **35**
Billington. *Beds* 2B **6**
Bilsham. *W Sus* 2B **44**
Bilsington. *Kent* 2A **40**
Bilting. *Kent* 1A **40**
Bines Green. *W Sus* 1D **45**
Binfield. *Brac* 1A **24**
Binfield Heath. *Oxon* 1D **23**
Binley. *Hants* 3A **22**
Binstead. *IOW* 3B **42**
Binstead. *W Sus* 2B **44**
Binsted. *Hants* 1D **33**
Birch. *Essx* 3D **11**
Birchanger. *Essx* 2D **9**
Birch Green. *Essx* 3D **11**
Birchington. *Kent* 2C **31**
Birchmoor Green. *Beds* 1B **6**
Birdbrook. *Essx* 1B **10**
Birdham. *W Sus* 2A **44**
Birds Green. *Essx* 1D **19**
Birling. *Kent* 2A **28**
Birling Gap. *E Sus* 3D **47**
Bisham. *Wind* 3A **16**
Bishopsbourne. *Kent* 3B **30**
Bishop's Green. *Essx* 3A **10**
Bishop's Green. *Hants* 2B **22**
Bishops Sutton. *Hants* 2C **33**
Bishopstoke. *Hants* 1A **42**
Bishopstone. *Buck* 3A **6**
Bishopstone. *E Sus* 2C **47**
Bishop's Waltham. *Hants* 1B **42**
Bisley. *Surr* 3B **24**
Bitterne. *Sotn* 1A **42**
Bix. *Oxon* 3D **15**
Blackboys. *E Sus* 3D **37**
Blackbrook. *Surr* 1D **35**
Blackditch. *Oxon* 1A **14**
Blackfen. *G Lon* 1C **27**
Blackfield. *Hants* 2A **42**
Blackham. *E Sus* 2C **37**
Blackheath. *Essx* 2A **12**
Blackheath. *G Lon* 1B **26**
Blackheath. *Surr* 1C **35**
Blackmoor. *Hants* 2D **33**
Blackmore. *Essx* 1A **20**
Blackmore End. *Essx* 1B **10**
Blackmore End. *Herts* 3D **7**
Blacknest. *Hants* 1D **33**
Black Notley. *Essx* 2B **10**
Blackstone. *W Sus* 1A **46**
Blackthorn. *Oxon* 3C **5**
Blackwall Tunnel. *G Lon* 3B **18**
Blackwater. *Hants* 3A **24**
Blackwater. *IOW* 3B **42**
Bladon. *Oxon* 3A **4**
Blake End. *Essx* 2B **10**
Blean. *Kent* 2B **30**
Bledlow. *Buck* 1D **15**
Bledlow Ridge. *Buck* 2D **15**
Blendworth. *Hants* 1D **43**
Blenheim. *Oxon* 1B **14**
Bletchingdon. *Oxon* 3B **4**
Bletchingley. *Surr* 3B **26**
Bletchley. *Mil* 1A **6**
Blewbury. *Oxon* 3B **14**
Blindley Heath. *Surr* 1B **36**
Bloxham. *Oxon* 1A **4**
Blue Bell Hill. *Kent* 2B **28**
Blue Row. *Essx* 3A **12**
Bluetown. *Kent* 3D **29**
Boarhunt. *Hants* 2C **43**
Boarshead. *E Sus* 2D **37**
Boars Hill. *Oxon* 1A **14**
Boarstall. *Buck* 3C **5**
Bobbing. *Kent* 2C **29**
Bobbingworth. *Essx* 1D **19**
Bocking. *Essx* 2B **10**

Bocking Churchstreet. *Essx* 2B **10**
Bodiam. *E Sus* 3B **38**
Bodicote. *Oxon* 1A **4**
Bodle Street Green. *E Sus* 1A **48**
Bodsham Green. *Kent* 1B **40**
Bognor Regis. *W Sus* 3B **44**
Bolney. *W Sus* 3A **36**
Bonnington. *Kent* 2A **40**
Booker. *Buck* 2A **16**
Boorley Green. *Hants* 1B **42**
Borden. *Kent* 2C **29**
Borden. *W Sus* 3A **34**
Bordon. *Hants* 2A **34**
Boreham. *Essx* 1B **20**
Boreham Street. *E Sus* 1A **48**
Borehamwood. *Herts* 2D **17**
Borley. *Essx* 1C **11**
Borley Green. *Essx* 1C **11**
Borough Green. *Kent* 3A **28**
Borstal. *Medw* 2B **28**
Bosham. *W Sus* 2A **44**
Bossingham. *Kent* 1B **40**
Botany Bay. *G Lon* 2A **18**
Bothampstead. *W Ber* 1B **22**
Botley. *Buck* 1B **16**
Botley. *Hants* 1B **42**
Botley. *Oxon* 1A **14**
Botolph Claydon. *Buck* 2D **5**
Botolphs. *W Sus* 2D **45**
Bough Beech. *Kent* 1C **37**
Boughton Aluph. *Kent* 1A **40**
Boughton Green. *Kent* 3B **28**
Boughton Lees. *Kent* 1A **40**
Boughton Malherbe. *Kent* 1C **39**
Boughton Monchelsea. *Kent* .. 3B **28**
Boughton under Blean. *Kent* .. 3A **30**
Bouldnor. *IOW* 3A **42**
Bourne End. *Buck* 3A **16**
Bourne End. *Herts* 1C **17**
Bournes Green. *S'end* 3D **21**
Bourne, The. *Surr* 1A **34**
Boveney. *Buck* 1B **24**
Bovingdon. *Herts* 1C **17**
Bovingdon Green. *Buck* 3A **16**
Bovinger. *Essx* 1D **19**
Bow Brickhill. *Mil* 1B **6**
Bowcombe. *IOW* 3A **42**
Bowers Gifford. *Essx* 3B **20**
Bowlhead Green. *Surr* 2B **34**
Boxford. *Suff* 1D **11**
Boxford. *W Ber* 1A **22**
Boxgrove. *W Sus* 2B **44**
Boxley. *Kent* 3B **28**
Boxted. *Essx* 1D **11**
Boxted Cross. *Essx* 1A **12**
Boyden Gate. *Kent* 2C **31**
Boyton Cross. *Essx* 1A **20**
Boyton End. *Essx* 1A **10**
Brabourne. *Kent* 1B **40**
Brabourne Lees. *Kent* 1A **40**
Bracklesham. *W Sus* 3A **44**
Brackley. *Nptn* 1B **4**
Brackley Hatch. *Nptn* 1C **5**
Bracknell. *Brac* 2A **24**
Bradenham. *Buck* 2A **16**
Bradfield. *Essx* 1B **12**
Bradfield. *W Ber* 1C **23**
Bradfield Heath. *Essx* 2B **12**
Brading. *IOW* 3C **43**
Bradley. *Hants* 1C **33**
Bradwell. *Essx* 2C **11**
Bradwell. *Mil* 1A **6**
Bradwell-on-Sea. *Essx* 3A **12**
Bradwell Waterside. *Essx* .. 1D **21**
Bragbury End. *Herts* 2A **8**
Braintree. *Essx* 2B **10**
Braishfield. *Hants* 3A **32**
Bramber. *W Sus* 1D **45**
Brambledown. *Kent* 1D **29**
Brambridge. *Hants* 3A **32**
Bramdean. *Hants* 3C **33**
Bramfield. *Herts* 3A **8**
Bramley. *Hants* 3C **23**
Bramley. *Surr* 1C **35**
Bramley Green. *Hants* 3C **23**
Bramling. *Kent* 3C **31**
Bramshill. *Hants* 2D **23**
Bramshott. *Hants* 2A **34**
Bran End. *Essx* 2A **10**
Bransbury. *Hants* 1A **32**
Brantham. *Suff* 1B **12**
Brasted. *Kent* 3C **27**
Brasted Chart. *Kent* 3C **27**
Braughing. *Herts* 2B **8**
Bray. *Wind* 1B **24**
Bray Wick. *Wind* 1A **24**
Breach. *W Sus* 2D **43**
Breachwood Green. *Herts* . 2D **7**
Brede. *E Sus* 1C **49**
Bredgar. *Kent* 2C **29**
Bredhurst. *Kent* 2B **28**
Brenchley. *Kent* 1A **38**
Brent Cross. *G Lon* 3A **18**
Brentford. *G Lon* 1D **25**
Brent Pelham. *Herts* 1C **9**

Brentwood. *Essx* 2A **20**
Brenzett. *Kent* 3A **40**
Brewer Street. *Surr* 3B **26**
Bricket Wood. *Herts* 1D **17**
Bridge. *Kent* 3B **30**
Bridge Green. *Essx* 1C **9**
Bridgemary. *Hants* 2B **42**
Brighthampton. *Oxon* 1A **14**
Brightling. *E Sus* 3A **38**
Brightlingsea. *Essx* 3A **12**
Brighton. *Brig* .... 2B **46** & **62**
Brighton Hill. *Hants* 1C **33**
Brightwalton. *W Ber* 1A **22**
Brightwalton Green. *W Ber* ... 1A **22**
Brightwell. *Suff* 1C **13**
Brightwell Baldwin. *Oxon* 2C **15**
Brightwell-cum-Sotwell. *Oxon* . 2B **14**
Brill. *Buck* 3C **5**
Brimpton. *W Ber* 2B **22**
Brissenden Green. *Kent* 2D **39**
Britwell Salome. *Oxon* 2C **15**
Brixton. *G Lon* 1B **26**
Broadbridge. *W Sus* 2A **44**
Broadbridge Heath. *W Sus* ... 2D **35**
Broadfield. *W Sus* 2A **36**
Broadford Bridge. *W Sus* 3C **35**
Broad Green. *Beds* 1B **6**
Broad Laying. *Hants* 2A **22**
Broadley Common. *Essx* 1C **19**
Broadmere. *Hants* 1C **33**
Broad Oak. *E Sus* 1C **49**
                (nr. Hastings)
Broad Oak. *E Sus* 3A **38**
                (nr. Heathfield)
Broadoak. *Hants* 1A **42**
Broad Oak. *Kent* 2B **30**
Broad's Green. *Essx* 3A **10**
Broadstairs. *Kent* 2D **31**
Broad Street. *E Sus* 1A **48**
Broad Street. *Kent* 1B **40**
                (nr. Ashford)
Broad Street. *Kent* 3C **29**
                (nr. Maidstone)
Broad Street Green. *Essx* .. 1C **21**
Brockbridge. *Hants* 1C **43**
Brockham. *Surr* 1D **35**
Brockhurst. *Hants* 2B **42**
Brogborough. *Beds* 1B **6**
Bromley. *G Lon* 2C **27**
Bromley. *Herts* 2C **9**
Bromley Green. *Kent* 2D **39**
Brompton. *Medw* 2B **28**
Brook. *Kent* 1A **40**
Brook. *Surr* 1C **35**
                (nr. Guildford)
Brook. *Surr* 2B **34**
                (nr. Haslemere)
Brookland. *Kent* 3D **39**
Brookmans Park. *Herts* ... 1A **18**
Brooks Green. *W Sus* 3D **35**
Brook Street. *Essx* 2D **19**
Brook Street. *Kent* 2D **37**
Brook Street. *W Sus* 3B **36**
Brookwood. *Surr* 3B **24**
Broom. *Beds* 1D **7**
Broomer's Corner. *W Sus* . 3D **35**
Broomfield. *Essx* 3B **10**
Broomfield. *Kent* 2B **30**
                (nr. Herne Bay)
Broomfield. *Kent* 3C **29**
                (nr. Maidstone)
Broomhall. *Wind* 2B **24**
Broughton. *Mil* 1A **6**
Broughton. *Oxon* 1A **4**
Brownbread Street. *E Sus* . 1A **48**
Brown Candover. *Hants* .. 2B **32**
Broxbourne. *Herts* 1B **18**
Broxted. *Essx* 2D **9**
Broyle Side. *E Sus* 1C **47**
Bryant's Bottom. *Buck* .. 2A **16**
Buckhurst Hill. *Essx* 2C **19**
Buckingham. *Buck* 1C **5**
Buckland. *Buck* 3A **6**
Buckland. *Herts* 1B **8**
Buckland. *Kent* 1D **41**
Buckland. *Oxon* 3A **26**
Buckland. *Surr* 3A **26**
Buckland Common. *Buck* . 1B **16**
Bucklebury. *W Ber* 1B **22**
Bucklers Hard. *Hants* ... 3A **42**
Bucklesham. *Suff* 1C **13**
Bucknell. *Oxon* 2B **4**
Bucks Green. *W Sus* 2C **35**
Bucks Hill. *Herts* 1C **17**
Bucks Horn Oak. *Hants* . 1A **34**
Buffler's Holt. *Buck* 1C **5**
Bulbourne. *Herts* 3B **6**
Bull's Green. *Herts* 3A **8**
Bulmer. *Essx* 1C **11**
Bulmer Tye. *Essx* 1C **11**
Bulphan. *Thur* 3A **20**
Bulverhythe. *E Sus* 2B **48**
Bumble's Green. *Essx* .. 1C **19**
Buntingford. *Herts* 2B **8**
Buntings Green. *Essx* .. 1C **11**

Burchett's Green. *Wind* 3A **16**
Burcot. *Oxon* 2B **14**
Burcott. *Buck* 2A **6**
Burdrop. *Oxon* 1A **4**
Bures. *Suff* 1D **11**
Burgess Hill. *W Sus* 1B **46**
Burghclere. *Hants* 2A **22**
Burghfield. *W Ber* 2C **23**
Burghfield Common. *W Ber* 2C **23**
Burghfield Hill. *W Ber* 2C **23**
Burgh Heath. *Surr* 3A **26**
Burham. *Kent* 2B **28**
Buriton. *Hants* 3D **33**
Burleigh. *Brac* 1B **24**
Burmarsh. *Kent* 2B **40**
Burnbrook. *Kent* 3B **16**
Burnham Green. *Herts* 3A **8**
Burnham-on-Crouch. *Essx* 2D **21**
Burntcommon. *Surr* 3C **25**
Burnt Heath. *Essx* 2A **12**
Burnt Hill. *W Ber* 1B **22**
Burnt Oak. *G Lon* 2A **18**
Burpham. *Surr* 3C **25**
Burpham. *W Sus* 2C **45**
Burridge. *Hants* 1B **42**
Burrowhill. *Surr* 2B **24**
Bursledon. *Hants* 2A **42**
Burstow. *Surr* 1B **36**
Burton End. *Essx* 2D **9**
Burton's Green. *Essx* 2C **11**
Burwash. *E Sus* 3A **38**
Burwash Common. *E Sus* ... 3A **38**
Burwash Weald. *E Sus* 3A **38**
Bury. *W Sus* 1C **45**
Bury Green. *Herts* 2C **9**
Busbridge. *Surr* 1B **34**
Bushey. *Herts* 2D **17**
Bushey Heath. *Herts* 2D **17**
Bustard Green. *Essx* 2A **10**
Butcher's Cross. *E Sus* 3D **37**
Buttsash. *Hants* 2A **42**
Butt's Green. *Essx* 1B **20**
Buxted. *E Sus* 3C **37**
Bybrook. *Kent* 1A **40**
Byfleet. *Surr* 2C **25**
Bygrave. *Herts* 1A **8**
Byworth. *W Sus* 3B **34**

C

Caddington. *Beds* 3C **7**
Cade Street. *E Sus* 3A **38**
Cadmore End. *Buck* 2D **15**
Cadwell. *Herts* 1D **7**
Calais Street. *Suff* 1D **11**
Calbourne. *IOW* 3A **42**
Calcot Row. *W Ber* 1C **23**
Calcott. *Kent* 2B **30**
Caldecote. *Herts* 1A **8**
Caldecott. *Oxon* 2A **14**
Calshot. *Hants* 2A **42**
Calvert. *Buck* 2C **5**
Calverton. *Mil* 1D **5**
Camber. *E Sus* 1D **49**
Camberley. *Surr* 2A **24**
Camberwell. *G Lon* 1B **26**
Camden Town. *G Lon* 3A **18**
Camelsdale. *Surr* 2B **34**
Camps End. *Cambs* 1A **10**
Campton. *Beds* 1D **7**
Canadia. *E Sus* 1B **48**
Cane End. *Oxon* 1C **23**
Canewdon. *Essx* 2C **21**
Canterbury. *Kent* ... 3B **30** & **63**
Cantley. *Essx* 3B **20**
Capel. *Kent* 1A **38**
Capel. *Surr* 1D **35**
Capel-le-Ferne. *Kent* 2C **41**
Capel St Mary. *Suff* 1A **12**
Carisbrooke. *IOW* 3A **42**
Carshalton. *G Lon* 1A **26**
Cartbridge. *Surr* 3C **25**
Cassington. *Oxon* 3A **4**
Castle Camps. *Cambs* 1A **10**
Castle Green. *Surr* 2B **24**
Castle Hedingham. *Essx* .. 1B **10**
Castle Hill. *Kent* 1A **38**
Caterham. *Surr* 3B **26**
Catford. *G Lon* 1B **26**
Catherington. *Hants* 1C **43**
Catisfield. *Hants* 2B **42**
Catmore. *W Ber* 3A **14**
Catsfield. *E Sus* 1B **48**
Cattawade. *Suff* 1B **12**
Catteshall. *Surr* 1B **34**
Caulcott. *Oxon* 2B **4**
Caversfield. *Oxon* 2B **4**
Caversham. *Read* 1D **23**
Caversham Heights. *Read* . 1C **23**
Chackmore. *Buck* 1C **5**
Chacombe. *Nptn* 1A **4**
Chaddleworth. *W Ber* ... 1A **22**
Chadwell Heath. *G Lon* . 3C **19**
Chadwell St Mary. *Thur* . 1A **28**

Chafford Hundred. *Thur* 1A **28**
Chailey. *E Sus* 1B **46**
Chainhurst. *Kent* 1B **38**
Chaldon. *Surr* 3B **26**
Chalfont Common. *Buck* 2C **17**
Chalfont St Giles. *Buck* 2B **16**
Chalfont St Peter. *Buck* 3C **17**
Chalgrove. *Oxon* 2C **15**
Chalk. *Kent* 1A **28**
Chalk End. *Essx* 3A **10**
Challock. *Kent* 3A **30**
Chalton. *Beds* 2C **7**
Chalton. *Hants* 1D **43**
Chalvington. *E Sus* 2D **47**
Chandler's Cross. *Herts* 2C **17**
Chandler's Ford. *Hants* 3A **32**
Channel Tunnel. *Kent* 2B **40**
Chantry. *Suff* 1B **12**
Chapel End. *Beds* 1C **7**
Chapel Row. *W Ber* 2B **22**
Chapmore End. *Herts* 3B **8**
Chappel. *Essx* 2C **11**
Charing. *Kent* 1D **39**
Charing Heath. *Kent* 1D **39**
Charing Hill. *Kent* 3D **29**
Charlbury. *Oxon* 3A **4**
Charleshill. *Surr* 1A **34**
Charlton. *G Lon* 1C **27**
Charlton. *Hants* 1A **32**
Charlton. *Herts* 2D **7**
Charlton. *Nptn* 1B **4**
Charlton. *Oxon* 3A **14**
Charlton. *W Sus* 1A **44**
Charlton-on-Otmoor. *Oxon* 3B **4**
Charlwood. *Hants* 2C **33**
Charlwood. *Surr* 1A **36**
Charndon. *Buck* 2C **5**
Charney Bassett. *Oxon* 2A **14**
Chart Corner. *Kent* 3B **28**
Charter Alley. *Hants* 3B **22**
Chartham. *Kent* 3B **30**
Chartham Hatch. *Kent* 3B **30**
Chartridge. *Buck* 1B **16**
Chart Sutton. *Kent* 3B **28**
Chart, The. *Kent* 3C **27**
Charvil. *Wok* 1D **23**
Chatham. *Medw* 2B **28**
Chatham Green. *Essx* 3B **10**
Chattenden. *Medw* 1B **28**
Chattisham. *Suff* 1A **12**
Chaulden. *Herts* 1C **17**
Chaul End. *Beds* 2C **7**
Chawley. *Oxon* 1A **14**
Chawton. *Hants* 2D **33**
Cheam. *Surr* 2A **26**
Cheapside. *Wind* 2B **24**
Chearsley. *Buck* 3D **5**
Checkendon. *Oxon* 3C **15**
Cheddington. *Buck* 3B **6**
Cheeseman's Green. *Kent* 2A **40**
Chelmondiston. *Suff* 1C **13**
Chelmsford. *Essx* 1B **20**
Chelsea. *G Lon* 1A **26**
Chelsfield. *G Lon* 2C **27**
Chelsham. *Surr* 3B **26**
Chelwood Common. *E Sus* 3C **37**
Chelwood Gate. *E Sus* 3C **37**
Chenies. *Buck* 2C **17**
Cheriton. *Hants* 3B **32**
Cheriton. *Kent* 2C **41**
Cherry Green. *Herts* 2B **8**
Chertsey. *Surr* 2C **25**
Chesham. *Buck* 1B **16**
Chesham Bois. *Buck* 2B **16**
Cheshunt. *Herts* 1B **18**
Chessington. *G Lon* 2D **25**
Chesterton. *Oxon* 2B **4**
Chestfield. *Kent* 2B **30**
Chetwode. *Buck* 2C **5**
Chevening. *Kent* 3C **27**
Chichester. *W Sus* 2A **44**
Chidden. *Hants* 1C **43**
Chiddingfold. *Surr* 2B **34**
Chiddingly. *E Sus* 1D **47**
Chiddingstone. *Kent* 1C **37**
Chiddingstone Causeway. *Kent* . . . 1D **37**
Chiddingstone Hoath. *Kent* 1C **37**
Chidham. *W Sus* 2D **43**
Chieveley. *W Ber* 1A **22**
Chignall St James. *Essx* 1A **20**
Chignall Smealy. *Essx* 3A **10**
Chigwell. *Essx* 2C **19**
Chigwell Row. *Essx* 2C **19**
Chilbolton. *Hants* 1A **32**
Chilcomb. *Hants* 3B **32**
Childrey. *Oxon* 3A **14**
Childwick Green. *Herts* 3D **7**
Chilgrove. *W Sus* 1A **44**
Chilham. *Kent* 3A **30**
Chilland. *Hants* 2B **32**
Chillenden. *Kent* 3C **31**
Chilmington Green. *Kent* 1D **39**
Chiltern Green. *Beds* 3D **7**
Chilton. *Buck* 3C **5**
Chilton. *Oxon* 3A **14**

Chilton Candover. *Hants* 1B **32**
Chilworth. *Hants* 1A **42**
Chilworth. *Surr* 1C **35**
Chimney. *Oxon* 1A **14**
Chineham. *Hants* 3C **23**
Chingford. *G Lon* 2B **18**
Chinnor. *Oxon* 1D **15**
Chipperfield. *Herts* 1C **17**
Chipping. *Herts* 1B **8**
Chipping Hill. *Essx* 3C **11**
Chipping Ongar. *Essx* 1D **19**
Chipstead. *Kent* 3D **27**
Chipstead. *Surr* 3A **26**
Chisbridge Cross. *Buck* 3A **16**
Chislehampton. *Oxon* 2B **14**
Chislehurst. *G Lon* 2C **27**
Chislet. *Kent* 2C **31**
Chiswell Green. *Herts* 1D **17**
Chiswick. *G Lon* 1A **26**
Chitcombe. *E Sus* 3C **39**
Chithurst. *W Sus* 3A **34**
Chobham. *Surr* 2B **24**
Cholesbury. *Buck* 1B **16**
Cholsey. *Oxon* 3B **14**
Chorleywood. *Herts* 2C **17**
Chrishall. *Essx* 1C **9**
Christmas Common. *Oxon* 2D **15**
Chuck Hatch. *E Sus* 2C **37**
Church Common. *Hants* 3D **33**
Church Crookham. *Hants* 3A **24**
Church End. *Beds* 2B **6**
(nr. Dunstable)
Church End. *Beds* 1D **7**
(nr. Stotfold)
Church End. *Beds* 1B **6**
(nr. Woburn)
Church End. *Essx* 2B **10**
(nr. Braintree)
Churchend. *Essx* 2A **10**
(nr. Great Dunmow)
Church End. *Essx* 1D **9**
(nr. Saffron Walden)
Churchend. *Essx* 2D **21**
(nr. Southend)
Church End. *Hants* 3C **23**
Church Enstone. *Oxon* 2A **4**
Church Hanborough. *Oxon* 3A **4**
Church Hougham. *Kent* 1C **41**
Church Langley. *Essx* 1C **19**
Church Norton. *W Sus* 3A **44**
Church Street. *Kent* 1B **28**
Churt. *Surr* 2A **34**
Cippenham. *Slo* 3B **16**
City (London) Airport. *G Lon* 3C **19**
City of London. *G Lon* 3B **18**
City, The. *Buck* 2D **15**
Clacton-on-Sea. *Essx* 3B **12**
Clanfield. *Hants* 1C **43**
Clapgate. *Herts* 2C **9**
Clapham. *G Lon* 1A **26**
Clapham. *W Sus* 2C **45**
Clap Hill. *Kent* 2A **40**
Clark's Green. *Surr* 2D **35**
Clatterford. *IOW* 3A **42**
Clavering. *Essx* 1C **9**
Clay End. *Herts* 2B **8**
Claygate. *Kent* 1B **38**
Claygate. *Surr* 2D **25**
Claygate Cross. *Kent* 3A **28**
Clayhall. *Hants* 3C **43**
Clayhill. *E Sus* 3C **39**
Clayton. *W Sus* 1B **46**
Cleeve. *Oxon* 3C **15**
Cleveley. *Oxon* 2A **4**
Cliddesden. *Hants* 1C **33**
Cliffe. *Medw* 1B **28**
Cliff End. *E Sus* 1C **49**
Cliffe Woods. *Medw* 1B **28**
Cliffs End. *Kent* 2D **31**
Clifton. *Beds* 1D **7**
Clifton. *Oxon* 1A **4**
Clifton Hampden. *Oxon* 2B **14**
Cliftonville. *Kent* 1D **31**
Climping. *W Sus* 2B **44**
Clophill. *Beds* 1C **7**
Clothall. *Herts* 1A **8**
Coalhill. *Essx* 2B **20**
Coates. *W Sus* 1B **44**
Cobham. *Kent* 2A **28**
Cobham. *Surr* 2D **25**
Cock Clarks. *Essx* 1C **21**
Cockernhoe. *Herts* 2D **7**
Cockfosters. *G Lon* 2A **18**
Cock Green. *Essx* 3A **10**
Cocking. *W Sus* 1A **44**
Cocking Causeway. *W Sus* 1A **44**
Cockpole Green. *Wind* 3A **16**
Codicote. *Herts* 3A **8**
Codmore Hill. *W Sus* 3C **35**
Cogges. *Oxon* 1A **14**
Coggeshall. *Essx* 2C **11**
Coggeshall Hamlet. *Essx* 2C **11**
Coggins Mill. *E Sus* 3D **37**
Colchester. *Essx* 2A **12**
Cold Ash. *W Ber* 2B **22**

Coldean. *Brig* 2B **46**
Colden Common. *Hants* 3A **32**
Coldharbour. *Kent* 3D **27**
Coldharbour. *Surr* 1D **35**
Cold Norton. *Essx* 1C **21**
Coldred. *Kent* 1C **41**
Coldwaltham. *W Sus* 1C **45**
Cole Green. *Herts* 3A **8**
Cole Henley. *Hants* 3A **22**
Coleman Green. *Herts* 3D **7**
Coleman's Hatch. *E Sus* 2C **37**
Colemore. *Hants* 2D **33**
Coleshill. *Buck* 2B **16**
Colgate. *W Sus* 3A **36**
Collier Row. *G Lon* 2C **19**
Colliers End. *Herts* 3B **8**
Collier Street. *Kent* 1B **38**
Colnbrook. *Slo* 1C **25**
Colne Engaine. *Essx* 1C **11**
Colney Heath. *Herts* 1A **18**
Colney Street. *Herts* 1D **17**
Colt's Hill. *Kent* 1A **38**
Colworth. *W Sus* 2B **44**
Combe. *Oxon* 3A **4**
Combe. *W Ber* 2A **22**
Combe Common. *Surr* 2B **34**
Compton. *Hants* 3A **32**
Compton. *Surr* 1B **34**
Compton. *W Ber* 3B **14**
Compton. *W Sus* 1D **43**
Coneyhurst Common. *W Sus* 3D **35**
Conford. *Hants* 2A **34**
Conyer. *Kent* 2D **29**
Cooden. *E Sus* 2B **48**
Cookham. *Wind* 3A **16**
Cookham Dean. *Wind* 3A **16**
Cookham Rise. *Wind* 3A **16**
Cookley Green. *Oxon* 2C **15**
Cooksbridge. *E Sus* 1C **47**
Cooksmill Green. *Essx* 1A **20**
Coolham. *W Sus* 3D **35**
Cooling. *Medw* 1B **28**
Cooling Street. *Medw* 1B **28**
Coombe. *Hants* 3C **33**
Coombes. *W Sus* 2D **45**
Coopersale Common. *Essx* 1C **19**
Coopersale Street. *Essx* 1C **19**
Cooper's Corner. *Kent* 1C **37**
Cooper Street. *Kent* 3D **31**
Cootham. *W Sus* 1C **45**
Copdock. *Suff* 1B **12**
Copford. *Essx* 2D **11**
Copford Green. *Essx* 2D **11**
Copsale. *W Sus* 3D **35**
Copthall Green. *Essx* 1C **19**
Copthorne. *W Sus* 2B **36**
Corhampton. *Hants* 3C **33**
Cornish Hall End. *Essx* 1A **10**
Corringham. *Thur* 3B **20**
Coryton. *Thur* 3B **20**
Coscote. *Oxon* 3B **14**
Cosgrove. *Nptn* 1D **5**
Cosham. *Port* 2C **43**
Cote. *Oxon* 1A **14**
Cothill. *Oxon* 2A **14**
Cottered. *Herts* 2B **8**
Cottisford. *Oxon* 1B **4**
Coulsdon. *Surr* 3A **26**
Coultershaw Bridge. *W Sus* 1B **44**
Countess Cross. *Essx* 1C **11**
Court-at-Street. *Kent* 2A **40**
Courtsend. *Essx* 2D **21**
Cousley Wood. *E Sus* 2A **38**
Cove. *Hants* 3A **24**
Cowbeech. *E Sus* 1A **48**
Cowden. *Kent* 1C **37**
Cowes. *IOW* 3A **42**
Cowfold. *W Sus* 3A **36**
Cowley. *G Lon* 3C **17**
Cowley. *Oxon* 1B **14**
Cowplain. *Hants* 1C **43**
Cox Green. *Surr* 2C **35**
Coxheath. *Kent* 3B **28**
Crabtree. *W Sus* 3A **36**
Crafton. *Buck* 3A **6**
Cranbourne. *Brac* 1B **24**
Cranbrook. *Kent* 2B **38**
Cranbrook Common. *Kent* 2B **38**
Cranfield. *Beds* 1B **6**
Cranford. *G Lon* 1C **25**
Cranham. *G Lon* 3D **19**
Cranleigh. *Surr* 2C **35**
Cranmore. *IOW* 3A **42**
Crawley. *Hants* 2A **32**
Crawley. *W Sus* 2A **36**
Crawley Down. *W Sus* 2B **36**
Crayford. *G Lon* 1D **27**
Crays Hill. *Essx* 2B **20**
Cray's Pond. *Oxon* 3C **15**
Crazies Hill. *Wok* 3D **15**
Creekmouth. *G Lon* 3C **19**
Cressing. *Essx* 2B **10**
Crews Hill. *G Lon* 1B **18**
Cricket Hill. *Hants* 2A **24**
Cricklewood. *G Lon* 3A **18**

Cripp's Corner. *E Sus* 3B **38**
Crockenhill. *Kent* 2D **27**
Crocker End. *Oxon* 3D **15**
Crockerhill. *Hants* 2B **42**
Crockham Hill. *Kent* 3C **27**
Crockhurst Street. *Kent* 1A **38**
Crockleford Heath. *Essx* 2A **12**
Cromer. *Herts* 2A **8**
Crondall. *Hants* 1D **33**
Crookham. *W Ber* 2B **22**
Crookham Village. *Hants* 3D **23**
Cross-at-Hand. *Kent* 1B **38**
Crossbush. *W Sus* 2C **45**
Cross End. *Essx* 1C **11**
Cross in Hand. *E Sus* 3D **37**
Crouch. *Kent* 3A **28**
Croughton. *Nptn* 1B **4**
Crowborough. *E Sus* 2D **37**
Crowdhill. *Hants* 1A **42**
Crowfield. *Nptn* 1C **5**
Crow Green. *Essx* 2D **19**
Crowhurst. *E Sus* 1B **48**
Crowhurst. *Surr* 1B **36**
Crowhurst Lane End. *Surr* 1B **36**
Crowmarsh Gifford. *Oxon* 3C **15**
Crowthorne. *Brac* 2A **24**
Croxley Green. *Herts* 2C **17**
Croydon. *G Lon* 2B **26**
Crundale. *Kent* 1A **40**
Crux Easton. *Hants* 3A **22**
Cryers Hill. *Buck* 2A **16**
Crystal Palace. *G Lon* 1B **26**
Cublington. *Buck* 2A **6**
Cuckfield. *W Sus* 3B **36**
Cuddesdon. *Oxon* 1C **15**
Cuddington. *Buck* 3D **5**
Cudham. *G Lon* 3C **27**
Cudworth. *Surr* 1A **36**
Cuffley. *Herts* 1B **18**
Culham. *Oxon* 2B **14**
Culverstone Green. *Kent* 2A **28**
Cumberlow Green. *Herts* 1B **8**
Cumnor. *Oxon* 1A **14**
Cupernham. *Hants* 3A **32**
Curbridge. *Hants* 1B **42**
Curdridge. *Hants* 1B **42**
Curridge. *W Ber* 1A **22**
Curtisden Green. *Kent* 1B **38**
Cutlers Green. *Essx* 1D **9**
Cuxham. *Oxon* 2C **15**
Cuxton. *Medw* 2B **28**

D

Dadford. *Buck* 1C **5**
Dagenham. *G Lon* 3C **19**
Dagnall. *Buck* 3B **6**
Dallington. *E Sus* 1A **48**
Danaway. *Kent* 2C **29**
Danbury. *Essx* 1B **20**
Dane End. *Herts* 2B **8**
Danehill. *E Sus* 3C **37**
Daneshill. *Hants* 3C **23**
Daniel's Water. *Kent* 1D **39**
Darenth. *Kent* 1D **27**
Dargate. *Kent* 2A **30**
Dartford. *Kent* 1D **27**
Dartford Crossing. *Kent* 1D **27**
Dassels. *Herts* 2B **8**
Datchet. *Wind* 1B **24**
Datchworth. *Herts* 3A **8**
Datchworth Green. *Herts* 3A **8**
Dawesgreen. *Surr* 1A **36**
Daws Heath. *Essx* 3C **21**
Deal. *Kent* 3D **31**
Dean. *Hants* 1B **42**
(nr. Bishop's Waltham)
Dean. *Hants* 2A **32**
(nr. Winchester)
Deane. *Hants* 3B **22**
Deanlane End. *W Sus* 1D **43**
Deanshanger. *Nptn* 1D **5**
Debden. *Essx* 1D **9**
Debden Green. *Essx* 2C **19**
(nr. Loughton)
Debden Green. *Essx* 1D **9**
(nr. Saffron Walden)
Deddington. *Oxon* 1A **4**
Dedham. *Essx* 1A **12**
Dedham Heath. *Essx* 1A **12**
Deepcut. *Surr* 3B **24**
Delly End. *Oxon* 3A **4**
Delvin End. *Essx* 1B **10**
Denchworth. *Oxon* 2A **14**
Dengie. *Essx* 1D **21**
Denham. *Buck* 3C **17**
Denham Green. *Buck* 3C **17**
Denmead. *Hants* 1C **43**
Densole. *Kent* 1C **41**
Denstroude. *Kent* 2B **30**
Denton. *E Sus* 2C **47**
Denton. *Kent* 1C **41**
Denton. *Oxon* 1B **14**
Deptford. *G Lon* 1B **26**

Derringstone. *Kent* ... 1C **41**
Detling. *Kent* ... 3B **28**
Dial Green. *W Sus* ... 3B **34**
Dial Post. *W Sus* ... 1D **45**
Dibden. *Hants* ... 2A **42**
Dibden Purlieu. *Hants* ... 2A **42**
Didcot. *Oxon* ... 2B **14**
Didling. *W Sus* ... 1A **44**
Digswell. *Herts* ... 3A **8**
Dingleden. *Kent* ... 2C **39**
Dinton. *Buck* ... 3D **5**
Dipley. *Hants* ... 3D **23**
Dippenhall. *Surr* ... 1A **34**
Ditchling. *E Sus* ... 1B **46**
Ditton. *Kent* ... 3B **28**
Doddinghurst. *Essx* ... 2D **19**
Doddington. *Kent* ... 3D **29**
Dogmersfield. *Hants* ... 3D **23**
Donkey Town. *Surr* ... 2B **24**
Donnington. *W Ber* ... 2A **22**
Donnington. *W Sus* ... 2A **44**
Doomsday Green. *W Sus* ... 2D **35**
Dorchester. *Oxon* ... 2B **14**
Dorking. *Surr* ... 1D **35**
Dorking Tye. *Suff* ... 1D **11**
Dormansland. *Surr* ... 1C **37**
Dormans Park. *Surr* ... 1B **36**
Dorney. *Buck* ... 1B **24**
Dorton. *Buck* ... 3C **5**
Dover. *Kent* ... 1D **41** & **63**
Dovercourt. *Essx* ... 1C **13**
Doversgreen. *Surr* ... 1A **36**
Dowlesgreen. *Wok* ... 2A **24**
Downe. *G Lon* ... 2C **27**
Downend. *IOW* ... 3B **42**
Downend. *W Ber* ... 1A **22**
Downham. *Essx* ... 2B **20**
Downley. *Buck* ... 2A **16**
Downside. *Surr* ... 3D **25**
Dragons Green. *W Sus* ... 3D **35**
Draycot. *Oxon* ... 1C **15**
Drayton. *Oxon* ... 2A **14**
(nr. Abingdon)
Drayton. *Oxon* ... 1A **4**
(nr. Banbury)
Drayton. *Port* ... 2C **43**
Drayton Beauchamp. *Buck* ... 3B **6**
Drayton Parslow. *Buck* ... 2A **6**
Drayton St Leonard. *Oxon* ... 2B **14**
Drellingore. *Kent* ... 1C **41**
Droxford. *Hants* ... 1C **43**
Dry Sandford. *Oxon* ... 1A **14**
Dry Street. *Essx* ... 3A **20**
Duck End. *Essx* ... 2A **10**
Ducklington. *Oxon* ... 1A **14**
Duddenhoe End. *Essx* ... 1C **9**
Duddleswell. *E Sus* ... 3C **37**
Dulwich. *G Lon* ... 1B **26**
Dummer. *Hants* ... 1B **32**
Dumpford. *W Sus* ... 3A **34**
Duncton. *W Sus* ... 1B **44**
Dundridge. *Hants* ... 1B **42**
Dungate. *Kent* ... 3D **29**
Dungeness. *Kent* ... 3A **40**
Dunk's Green. *Kent* ... 3A **28**
Dunley. *Hants* ... 3A **22**
Dunsden Green. *Oxon* ... 1D **23**
Dunsfold. *Surr* ... 2C **35**
Dunsmore. *Buck* ... 1A **16**
Dunstable. *Beds* ... 2C **7**
Duns Tew. *Oxon* ... 2A **4**
Dunton. *Buck* ... 2A **6**
Dunton Green. *Kent* ... 3D **27**
Durgates. *E Sus* ... 2A **38**
Durley. *Hants* ... 1B **42**
Durley Street. *Hants* ... 1B **42**
Durrant Green. *Kent* ... 2C **39**
Durrants. *Hants* ... 1D **43**
Durrington. *W Sus* ... 2D **45**
Duton Hill. *Essx* ... 2A **10**
Duxford. *Oxon* ... 2A **14**
Dymchurch. *Kent* ... 3B **40**

E

Ealing. *G Lon* ... 3D **17**
Earley. *Wok* ... 1D **23**
Earls Colne. *Essx* ... 2C **11**
Earnley. *W Sus* ... 3A **44**
Eartham. *W Sus* ... 2B **44**
Easebourne. *W Sus* ... 3A **34**
Eashing. *Surr* ... 1B **34**
Easington. *Buck* ... 3C **5**
Easington. *Oxon* ... 1A **4**
(nr. Banbury)
Easington. *Oxon* ... 2C **15**
(nr. Watlington)
Easole Street. *Kent* ... 3C **31**
East Anton. *Hants* ... 1A **32**
East Ashling. *W Sus* ... 2A **44**
East Aston. *Hants* ... 1A **32**
East Barnet. *G Lon* ... 2A **18**
East Beach. *W Sus* ... 3A **44**

East Bedfont. *G Lon* ... 1C **25**
East Bergholt. *Suff* ... 1A **12**
East Blatchington. *E Sus* ... 2C **47**
East Boldre. *Hants* ... 2A **42**
Eastbourne. *E Sus* ... 3A **48** & **63**
East Burnham. *Buck* ... 3B **16**
Eastbury. *Herts* ... 2C **17**
Eastbury. *W Ber* ... 1A **22**
East Challow. *Oxon* ... 3A **14**
East Chiltington. *E Sus* ... 1B **46**
Eastchurch. *Kent* ... 1D **29**
East Clandon. *Surr* ... 3C **25**
East Claydon. *Buck* ... 2D **5**
Eastcote. *G Lon* ... 3D **17**
East Cowes. *IOW* ... 3B **42**
East Dean. *E Sus* ... 3D **47**
East Dean. *W Sus* ... 1B **44**
East End. *Hants* ... 3A **42**
(nr. Lymington)
East End. *Hants* ... 2A **22**
(nr. Newbury)
East End. *Herts* ... 2C **9**
East End. *Kent* ... 1D **29**
(nr. Minster)
East End. *Kent* ... 2C **39**
(nr. Tenterden)
East End. *Oxon* ... 3A **4**
East End. *Suff* ... 1B **12**
Eastergate. *W Sus* ... 2B **44**
East Farleigh. *Kent* ... 3B **28**
East Garston. *W Ber* ... 1A **22**
East Ginge. *Oxon* ... 3A **14**
East Gores. *Essx* ... 2C **11**
East Grinstead. *W Sus* ... 2B **36**
East Guldeford. E Sus ... 3D **39**
East Hagbourne. Oxon ... 3B **14**
East Ham. *G Lon* ... 3C **19**
Easthampstead. *Brac* ... 2A **24**
East Hanney. *Oxon* ... 3A **14**
East Hanningfield. *Essx* ... 1B **20**
East Harting. *W Sus* ... 1A **44**
Eastheath. *Wok* ... 2A **24**
East Hendred. *Oxon* ... 3A **14**
East Hoathly. *E Sus* ... 1D **47**
Easthorpe. *Essx* ... 2D **11**
East Horsley. *Surr* ... 3C **25**
East Hyde. *Beds* ... 3D **7**
East Ilsley. *W Ber* ... 3A **14**
East Langdon. *Kent* ... 1D **41**
East Lavant. *W Sus* ... 2A **44**
East Lavington. *W Sus* ... 1B **44**
Eastleigh. *Hants* ... 1A **42**
Eastling. *Kent* ... 3D **29**
East Liss. *Hants* ... 3D **33**
East Lockinge. *Oxon* ... 3A **14**
East Malling. *Kent* ... 3B **28**
East Marden. *W Sus* ... 1A **44**
East Meon. *Hants* ... 3C **33**
East Mersea. *Essx* ... 3A **12**
East Molesey. *Surr* ... 2D **25**
Eastney. *Port* ... 3C **43**
East Oakley. *Hants* ... 3B **22**
Easton. *Hants* ... 2B **32**
East Peckham. *Kent* ... 1A **38**
East Preston. *W Sus* ... 2C **45**
Eastry. *Kent* ... 3D **31**
East Shefford. *W Ber* ... 1A **22**
East Stourmouth. *Kent* ... 2C **31**
East Stratton. *Hants* ... 1B **32**
East Studdal. *Kent* ... 1D **41**
East Tilbury. *Thur* ... 1A **28**
East Tisted. *Hants* ... 2D **33**
Eastwick. *Herts* ... 3C **9**
East Wittering. *W Sus* ... 3D **43**
Eastwood. *S'end* ... 3C **21**
East Woodhay. *Hants* ... 2A **22**
East Worldham. *Hants* ... 2D **33**
Eaton. *Oxon* ... 1A **14**
Eaton Bray. *Beds* ... 2B **6**
Ecchinswell. *Hants* ... 3B **22**
Eccles. *Kent* ... 2B **28**
Edburton. *W Sus* ... 1A **46**
Eddington. *Kent* ... 2B **30**
Eddington. *W Ber* ... 2A **22**
Edenbridge. *Kent* ... 1C **37**
Edgcott. *Buck* ... 2C **5**
Edgware. *G Lon* ... 2D **17**
Edlesborough. *Buck* ... 3B **6**
Edmonton. *G Lon* ... 2B **18**
Edney Common. *Essx* ... 1A **20**
Edwardstone. *Suff* ... 1D **11**
Edworth. *Beds* ... 1A **8**
Effingham. *Surr* ... 3D **25**
Effingham Common. *Surr* ... 3D **25**
Egbury. *Hants* ... 3A **22**
Egerton. *Kent* ... 1D **39**
Egerton Forstal. *Kent* ... 1C **39**
Eggington. *Beds* ... 2B **6**
Egham. *Surr* ... 1C **25**
Egham Hythe. *Surr* ... 1C **25**
Egypt. *Buck* ... 3B **16**
Egypt. *Hants* ... 1A **32**
Eight Ash Green. *Essx* ... 2D **11**
Elbridge. *W Sus* ... 2B **44**
Elcot. *W Ber* ... 2A **22**

Elder Street. *Essx* ... 1D **9**
Elham. *Kent* ... 1B **40**
Eling. *Hants* ... 1A **42**
Eling. *W Ber* ... 1B **22**
Elkins Green. *Essx* ... 1A **20**
Ellenbrook. *Herts* ... 1A **18**
Ellen's Green. *Surr* ... 2C **35**
Ellesborough. *Buck* ... 1A **16**
Ellisfield. *Hants* ... 1C **33**
Elmdon. *Essx* ... 1C **9**
Elmfield. *IOW* ... 3B **42**
Elm Park. *G Lon* ... 3D **19**
Elmstead. *Essx* ... 2A **12**
Elmstead Heath. *Essx* ... 2A **12**
Elmstead Market. *Essx* ... 2A **12**
Elmstone. *Kent* ... 2C **31**
Elsenham. *Essx* ... 2D **9**
Elsfield. *Oxon* ... 3B **4**
Elstead. *Surr* ... 1B **34**
Elsted. *W Sus* ... 1A **44**
Elsted Marsh. *W Sus* ... 3A **34**
Elstree. *Herts* ... 2D **17**
Eltham. *G Lon* ... 1C **27**
Elvetham Heath. *Hants* ... 3D **23**
Elvington. *Kent* ... 3C **31**
Embrook. *Wok* ... 2D **23**
Emmer Green. *Read* ... 1D **23**
Emmington. *Oxon* ... 1D **15**
Empshott. *Hants* ... 2D **33**
Emsworth. *Hants* ... 2D **43**
Enborne. *W Ber* ... 2A **22**
Enborne Row. *W Ber* ... 2A **22**
Enfield. *G Lon* ... 2B **18**
Enfield Wash. *G Lon* ... 2B **18**
Englefield. *W Ber* ... 1C **23**
Englefield Green. *Surr* ... 1B **24**
Enham Alamein. *Hants* ... 1A **32**
Enstone. *Oxon* ... 2A **4**
Epping. *Essx* ... 1C **19**
Epping Green. *Essx* ... 1C **19**
Epping Green. *Herts* ... 1A **18**
Epping Upland. *Essx* ... 1C **19**
Epsom. *Surr* ... 2A **26**
Epwell. *Oxon* ... 1A **4**
Eridge Green. *E Sus* ... 2D **37**
Erith. *G Lon* ... 1D **27**
Erriottwood. *Kent* ... 3D **29**
Erwarton. *Suff* ... 1C **13**
Esher. *Surr* ... 2D **25**
Essendon. *Herts* ... 1A **18**
Etchingham. *E Sus* ... 3B **38**
Etchinghill. *Kent* ... 2B **40**
Eton. *Wind* ... 1B **24**
Eton Wick. *Wind* ... 1B **24**
Evenley. *Nptn* ... 1B **4**
Eversholt. *Beds* ... 1B **6**
Eversley. *Hants* ... 2D **23**
Eversley Cross. *Hants* ... 2D **23**
Ewell. *Surr* ... 2A **26**
Ewell Minnis. *Kent* ... 1C **41**
Ewelme. *Oxon* ... 2C **15**
Ewhurst. *Surr* ... 1C **35**
Ewhurst Green. *E Sus* ... 3B **38**
Ewhurst Green. *Surr* ... 2C **35**
Ewshot. *Hants* ... 3A **24**
Exbury. *Hants* ... 2A **42**
Exceat. *E Sus* ... 3D **47**
Exlade Street. *Oxon* ... 3C **15**
Exton. *Hants* ... 3C **33**
Eyhorne Street. *Kent* ... 3C **29**
Eynsford. *Kent* ... 2D **27**
Eynsham. *Oxon* ... 1A **14**
Eythorne. *Kent* ... 1C **41**

F

Faccombe. *Hants* ... 3A **22**
Fairbourne Heath. *Kent* ... 3C **29**
Fairfield. *Kent* ... 3D **39**
Fairlands. *Surr* ... 3B **24**
Fairlight. *E Sus* ... 1C **49**
Fairlight Cove. *E Sus* ... 1C **49**
Fairmile. *Surr* ... 2D **25**
Fair Oak. *Hants* ... 1A **42**
(nr. Eastleigh)
Fair Oak. *Hants* ... 2B **22**
(nr. Kingsclere)
Fair Oak Green. *Hants* ... 2C **23**
Fairseat. *Kent* ... 2A **28**
Fairstead. *Essx* ... 3B **10**
Fairwarp. *E Sus* ... 3C **37**
Falkenham. *Suff* ... 1C **13**
Falmer. *E Sus* ... 2B **46**
Fancott. *Beds* ... 2C **7**
Fanner's Green. *Essx* ... 3A **10**
Fareham. *Hants* ... 2B **42**
Farleigh. *Surr* ... 2B **26**
Farleigh Wallop. *Hants* ... 1C **33**
Farley Green. *Surr* ... 1C **35**
Farley Hill. *Wok* ... 2D **23**
Farlington. *Port* ... 2C **43**
Farmoor. *Oxon* ... 1A **14**
Farnborough. *G Lon* ... 2C **27**

Farnborough. *Hants* ... 3A **24**
Farnborough. *W Ber* ... 3A **14**
Farnborough Airport. *Surr* ... 3A **24**
Farncombe. *Surr* ... 1B **34**
Farnham. *Essx* ... 2C **9**
Farnham. *Surr* ... 1A **34**
Farnham Common. *Buck* ... 3B **16**
Farnham Green. *Essx* ... 2C **9**
Farnham Royal. *Buck* ... 3B **16**
Farningham. *Kent* ... 2D **27**
Farthinghoe. *Nptn* ... 1B **4**
Faulkbourne. *Essx* ... 3B **10**
Faversham. *Kent* ... 2A **30**
Fawkham Green. *Kent* ... 2D **27**
Fawler. *Oxon* ... 3A **4**
Fawley. *Buck* ... 3D **15**
Fawley. *Hants* ... 2A **42**
Fawley. *W Ber* ... 3A **14**
Faygate. *W Sus* ... 2A **36**
Feering. *Essx* ... 2C **11**
Felbridge. *Surr* ... 2B **36**
Felcourt. *Surr* ... 1B **36**
Felden. *Herts* ... 1C **17**
Felixstowe. *Suff* ... 1C **13**
Felixstowe Ferry. *Suff* ... 1D **13**
Felpham. *W Sus* ... 3B **44**
Felsted. *Essx* ... 2A **10**
Feltham. *G Lon* ... 1D **25**
Felthamhill. *Surr* ... 1C **25**
Fencott. *Oxon* ... 3B **4**
Fenn Street. *Medw* ... 1B **28**
Fenny Stratford. *Mil* ... 1A **6**
Fernhill. *W Sus* ... 1A **36**
Fernhurst. *W Sus* ... 3A **34**
Ferring. *W Sus* ... 2D **45**
Fetcham. *Surr* ... 3D **25**
Fewcott. *Oxon* ... 2B **4**
Fiddlers Hamlet. *Essx* ... 1C **19**
Fifield. *Wind* ... 1B **24**
Finchampstead. *Wok* ... 2D **23**
Finchdean. *Hants* ... 1D **43**
Finchingfield. *Essx* ... 1A **10**
Finchley. *G Lon* ... 2A **18**
Findon. *W Sus* ... 2D **45**
Findon Valley. *W Sus* ... 2D **45**
Fingest. *Buck* ... 2D **15**
Finglesham. *Kent* ... 3D **31**
Fingringhoe. *Essx* ... 2A **12**
Finmere. *Oxon* ... 1C **5**
Finsbury. *G Lon* ... 3B **18**
Finstock. *Oxon* ... 3A **4**
Fishbourne. *IOW* ... 3B **42**
Fishbourne. *W Sus* ... 2A **44**
Fisher's Pond. *Hants* ... 3A **32**
Fisherstreet. *W Sus* ... 2B **34**
Fittleworth. *W Sus* ... 1C **45**
Five Ash Down. *E Sus* ... 3C **37**
Five Ashes. *E Sus* ... 3D **37**
Five Oak Green. *Kent* ... 1A **38**
Five Oaks. *W Sus* ... 3C **35**
Flack's Green. *Essx* ... 3B **10**
Flackwell Heath. *Buck* ... 3A **16**
Flamstead. *Herts* ... 3C **7**
Flansham. *W Sus* ... 2B **44**
Flaunden. *Herts* ... 1C **17**
Fleet. *Hants* ... 3A **24**
(nr. Farnborough)
Fleet. *Hants* ... 2D **43**
(nr. South Hayling)
Fleetville. *Herts* ... 1D **17**
Fletcher's Green. *Kent* ... 1D **37**
Fletching. *E Sus* ... 3C **37**
Flexford. *Surr* ... 3B **24**
Flimwell. *E Sus* ... 2B **38**
Flishinghurst. *Kent* ... 2B **38**
Flitton. *Beds* ... 1C **7**
Flitwick. *Beds* ... 1C **7**
Fobbing. *Thur* ... 3B **20**
Folkestone. *Kent* ... 2C **41** & **68**
Folkington. *E Sus* ... 2D **47**
Folly, The. *Herts* ... 3D **7**
Folly, The. *W Ber* ... 2A **22**
Fontwell. *W Sus* ... 2B **44**
Foots Cray. *G Lon* ... 1C **27**
Ford. *Buck* ... 1D **15**
Ford. *W Sus* ... 2C **45**
Fordcombe. *Kent* ... 1D **37**
Fordham. *Essx* ... 2D **11**
Fordham Heath. *Essx* ... 2D **11**
Ford Street. *Essx* ... 2D **11**
Fordwich. *Kent* ... 3B **30**
Forest Green. *Surr* ... 1D **35**
Forest Hill. *Oxon* ... 1B **14**
Forest Row. *E Sus* ... 2C **37**
Forestside. *W Sus* ... 1D **43**
Forstal, The. *Kent* ... 2A **40**
Forton. *Hants* ... 1A **32**
Forty Green. *Buck* ... 2B **16**
Forty Hill. *G Lon* ... 2B **18**
Foster Street. *Essx* ... 1C **19**
Foul Mile. *E Sus* ... 1A **48**
Four Elms. *Kent* ... 1C **37**
Four Marks. *Hants* ... 2C **33**
Four Oaks. *E Sus* ... 3C **39**

Four Throws—Hedgerley

Four Throws. *Kent* 3B **38**
Foxcombe Hill. *Oxon* 1A **14**
Fox Corner. *Surr* 3B **24**
Fox Hatch. *Essx* 2D **19**
Foxhunt Green. *E Sus* 1D **47**
Fox Lane. *Hants* 3A **24**
Fox Street. *Essx* 2A **12**
Framfield. *E Sus* 3C **37**
Frant. *E Sus* 2D **37**
Frating Green. *Essx* 2A **12**
Fratton. *Port* 2C **43**
Freefolk Priors. *Hants* 1A **32**
Freeland. *Oxon* 3A **4**
French Street. *Kent* 3C **27**
Frensham. *Surr* 1A **34**
Freshwater. *IOW* 3A **42**
Freston. *Suff* 1B **12**
Friar's Gate. *E Sus* 2C **37**
Friday Street. *E Sus* 2A **48**
Friday Street. *Surr* 1D **35**
Friern Barnet. *G Lon* 2A **18**
Frieth. *Buck* 2D **15**
Frilford. *Oxon* 2A **14**
Frilsham. *W Ber* 1B **22**
Frimley. *Surr* 3A **24**
Frimley Green. *Surr* 3A **24**
Frindsbury. *Medw* 2B **28**
Fringford. *Oxon* 2C **5**
Frinsted. *Kent* 3C **29**
Frinton-on-Sea. *Essx* 3C **13**
Friston. *E Sus* 3D **47**
Frithsden. *Herts* 1C **17**
Frittenden. *Kent* 1C **39**
Fritwell. *Oxon* 2B **4**
Frogham. *Kent* 3C **31**
Frogmore. *Hants* 2A **24**
Frogmore. *Herts* 1D **17**
Froxfield. *Beds* 1B **6**
Froxfield Green. *Hants* 3D **33**
Fryern Hill. *Hants* 3A **32**
Fryerning. *Essx* 1A **20**
Fulflood. *Hants* 2A **32**
Fulham. *G Lon* 1A **26**
Fulking. *W Sus* 1A **46**
Fuller Street. *Essx* 3B **10**
Fullerton. *Hants* 2A **32**
Fulmer. *Buck* 3B **16**
Funtington. *W Sus* 2A **44**
Funtley. *Hants* 2B **42**
Furner's Green. *E Sus* 3C **37**
Furneux Pelham. *Herts* 2C **9**
Furzeley Corner. *Hants* 1C **43**
Furzey Lodge. *Hants* 2A **42**
Fyfield. *Essx* 1D **19**
Fyfield. *Oxon* 2A **14**
Fyning. *W Sus* 3A **34**

G

Gadbrook. *Surr* 1A **36**
Gagingwell. *Oxon* 2A **4**
Gainsborough. *Suff* 1B **12**
Gainsford End. *Essx* 1B **10**
Galleyend. *Essx* 1B **20**
Galleywood. *Essx* 1B **20**
Gallowstree Common. *Oxon* 3C **15**
Gardeners Green. *Wok* 2A **24**
Garford. *Oxon* 2A **14**
Garlinge Green. *Kent* 3B **30**
Garsington. *Oxon* 1B **14**
Gatton. *Surr* 3A **26**
Gatwick (London) Airport. *W Sus* 1A **36**
Gawcott. *Buck* 1C **5**
Gay Bowers. *Essx* 1B **20**
Gay Street. *W Sus* 3C **35**
George Green. *Buck* 3B **16**
Gerrards Cross. *Buck* 3B **16**
Gestingthorpe. *Essx* 1C **11**
Gibraltar. *Buck* 3D **5**
Gidea Park. *G Lon* 3D **19**
Gillingham. *Medw* 2B **28**
Gill's Green. *Kent* 2B **38**
Glassenbury. *Kent* 2B **38**
Glympton. *Oxon* 2A **4**
Glynde. *E Sus* 2C **47**
Glyndebourne. *E Sus* 1C **47**
Goathurst Common. *Kent* 3C **27**
Goat Lees. *Kent* 1A **40**
Godalming. *Surr* 1B **34**
Goddard's Green. *Kent* 2C **39** (nr. Benenden)
Goddard's Green. *Kent* 2B **38** (nr. Cranbrook)
Goddards Green. *W Sus* 3A **36**
Godmersham. *Kent* 3A **30**
Godstone. *Surr* 3B **26**
Goff's Oak. *Herts* 1B **18**
Golden Cross. *E Sus* 1D **47**
Golden Green. *Kent* 1A **38**
Golden Pot. *Hants* 1D **33**
Golders Green. *G Lon* 3A **18**
Goldhanger. *Essx* 1D **21**
Goldstone. *Kent* 2C **31**
Gomshall. *Surr* 1C **35**
Good Easter. *Essx* 3A **10**
Goodmayes. *G Lon* 3C **19**
Goodnestone. *Kent* 3C **31** (nr. Aylesham)
Goodnestone. *Kent* 2A **30** (nr. Faversham)
Goodworth Clatford. *Hants* 1A **32**
Goosey. *Oxon* 2A **14**
Goring. *Oxon* 3C **15**
Goring-by-Sea. *W Sus* 2D **45**
Goring Heath. *Oxon* 1C **23**
Gosfield. *Essx* 2B **10**
Gosford. *Oxon* 3B **4**
Gosmore. *Herts* 2D **7**
Gosport. *Hants* 2C **43**
Gossops Green. *W Sus* 2A **36**
Goudhurst. *Kent* 2B **38**
Graffham. *W Sus* 1B **44**
Grafham. *Surr* 1C **35**
Grafty Green. *Kent* 1C **39**
Grain. *Medw* 1C **29**
Granborough. *Buck* 2D **5**
Grandpont. *Oxon* 1B **14**
Grange Hill. *G Lon* 2C **19**
Graveley. *Herts* 2A **8**
Graveney. *Kent* 2A **30**
Gravesend. *Kent* 1A **28**
Grays. *Thur* 1A **28**
Grayshott. *Hants* 2A **34**
Grayswood. *Surr* 2B **34**
Grazeley. *Wok* 2C **23**
Great Amwell. *Herts* 3B **8**
Great Baddow. *Essx* 1B **20**
Great Bardfield. *Essx* 1A **10**
Great Bentley. *Essx* 2B **12**
Great Bookham. *Surr* 3D **25**
Great Braxted. *Essx* 3C **11**
Great Brickhill. *Buck* 1B **6**
Great Bromley. *Essx* 2A **12**
Great Burstead. *Essx* 2A **20**
Great Canfield. *Essx* 3D **9**
Great Chart. *Kent* 1D **39**
Great Chesterford. *Essx* 1D **9**
Great Chishill. *Cambs* 1C **9**
Great Clacton. *Essx* 3B **12**
Great Cornard. *Suff* 1C **11**
Great Dunmow. *Essx* 2A **10**
Great Easton. *Essx* 2A **10**
Great Gaddesden. *Herts* 3C **7**
Great Hallingbury. *Essx* 3D **9**
Greatham. *Hants* 2D **33**
Greatham. *W Sus* 1C **45**
Great Hampden. *Buck* 1A **16**
Great Haseley. *Oxon* 1C **15**
Great Henny. *Essx* 1C **11**
Great Holland. *Essx* 3C **13**
Great Horkesley. *Essx* 1D **11**
Great Hormead. *Herts* 1C **9**
Great Horwood. *Buck* 1D **5**
Great Kimble. *Buck* 1A **16**
Great Kingshill. *Buck* 2A **16**
Great Leighs. *Essx* 3B **10**
Great Linford. *Mil* 1A **6**
Great Maplestead. *Essx* 1C **11**
Great Milton. *Oxon* 1C **15**
Great Missenden. *Buck* 1A **16**
Great Mongeham. *Kent* 3D **31**
Great Munden. *Herts* 2B **8**
Great Notley. *Essx* 2B **10**
Great Oakley. *Essx* 2B **12**
Great Offley. *Herts* 2D **7**
Great Oxney Green. *Essx* 1A **20**
Great Parndon. *Essx* 1C **19**
Great Saling. *Essx* 2A **10**
Great Sampford. *Essx* 1A **10**
Great Shefford. *W Ber* 1A **22**
Great Stambridge. *Essx* 2C **21**
Great Stonar. *Kent* 3D **31**
Greatstone-on-Sea. *Kent* 3A **40**
Great Tew. *Oxon* 2A **4**
Great Tey. *Essx* 2C **11**
Great Thorness. *IOW* 3A **42**
Great Totham North. *Essx* 3C **11**
Great Totham South. *Essx* 3C **11**
Great Wakering. *Essx* 3D **21**
Great Waldingfield. *Suff* 1D **11**
Great Waltham. *Essx* 3A **10**
Great Warley. *Essx* 2D **19**
Great Wenham. *Suff* 1A **12**
Great Wigborough. *Essx* 3D **11**
Greatworth. *Nptn* 1B **4**
Great Wymondley. *Herts* 2A **8**
Great Yeldham. *Essx* 1B **10**
Green End. *Herts* 1B **8** (nr. Buntingford)
Green End. *Herts* 2B **8** (nr. Stevenage)
Greenfield. *Beds* 1C **7**
Greenfield. *Oxon* 2D **15**
Greenford. *G Lon* 3D **17**
Greenham. *W Ber* 2A **22**
Greenhill. *Kent* 2B **30**
Greenhithe. *Kent* 1D **27**
Greenstead Green. *Essx* 2C **11**
Greensted Green. *Essx* 1D **19**
Green Street. *Herts* 2D **17**
Green Street Green. *G Lon* 2C **27**
Green Street Green. *Kent* 1D **27**
Green Tye. *Herts* 3C **9**
Greenwich. *G Lon* 1B **26**
Grendon Underwood. *Buck* 2C **5**
Greywell. *Hants* 3D **23**
Griggs Green. *Hants* 2A **34**
Grisling Common. *E Sus* 3C **37**
Groombridge. *E Sus* 2D **37**
Groton. *Suff* 1D **11**
Grove. *Kent* 2C **31**
Grove. *Oxon* 2A **14**
Grove Park. *G Lon* 1C **27**
Gubblecote. *Herts* 3B **6**
Guestling Green. *E Sus* 1C **49**
Guestling Thorn. *E Sus* 1C **49**
Guildford. *Surr* 1B **34** & **66**
Gundleton. *Hants* 2C **33**
Gun Green. *Kent* 2B **38**
Gun Hill. *E Sus* 1D **47**
Gunville. *IOW* 3A **42**
Gurnard. *IOW* 3A **42**
Guston. *Kent* 1D **41**

H

Habin. *W Sus* 3A **34**
Hackney. *G Lon* 3B **18**
Haddenham. *Buck* 1D **15**
Hadham Cross. *Herts* 3C **9**
Hadham Ford. *Herts* 2C **9**
Hadleigh. *Essx* 3C **21**
Hadleigh. *Suff* 1A **12**
Hadleigh Heath. *Suff* 1D **11**
Hadley Wood. *G Lon* 2A **18**
Hadlow. *Kent* 1A **38**
Hadlow Down. *E Sus* 3D **37**
Haffenden Quarter. *Kent* 1C **39**
Hailey. *Herts* 3B **8**
Hailey. *Oxon* 3A **4**
Hailsham. *E Sus* 2D **47**
Hainault. *G Lon* 2C **19**
Hale. *Surr* 1A **34**
Hale Street. *Kent* 1A **38**
Halfway. *W Ber* 2A **22**
Halfway Houses. *Kent* 1D **29**
Halland. *E Sus* 1D **47**
Halling. *Medw* 2B **28**
Hall's Green. *Herts* 2A **8**
Halnaker. *W Sus* 2B **44**
Halse. *Nptn* 1B **4**
Halstead. *Essx* 1C **11**
Halstead. *Kent* 2C **27**
Halton. *Buck* 1A **16**
Ham. *G Lon* 1D **25**
Ham. *Kent* 3D **31**
Hambleden. *Buck* 3D **15**
Hambledon. *Hants* 1C **43**
Hambledon. *Surr* 2B **34**
Hamble-le-Rice. *Hants* 2A **42**
Hambrook. *W Sus* 2D **43**
Ham Green. *Kent* 2C **29**
Ham Hill. *Kent* 2A **28**
Hammer. *W Sus* 2A **34**
Hammersmith. *G Lon* 1A **26**
Hammerwood. *E Sus* 2C **37**
Hammill. *Kent* 3C **31**
Hammond Street. *Herts* 1B **18**
Hampden Park. *E Sus* 2A **48**
Hamperden End. *Essx* 1D **9**
Hampstead. *G Lon* 3A **18**
Hampstead Norreys. *W Ber* 1B **22**
Hampton. *G Lon* 1D **25**
Hampton. *Kent* 2B **30**
Hampton Poyle. *Oxon* 3B **4**
Hampton Wick. *G Lon* 2D **25**
Hamsey. *E Sus* 1C **47**
Hamsey Green. *Surr* 3B **26**
Hamstead. *IOW* 3A **42**
Hamstead Marshall. *W Ber* 2A **22**
Hamstreet. *Kent* 2A **40**
Handcross. *W Sus* 3A **36**
Handy Cross. *Buck* 2A **16**
Hangleton. *Brig* 2A **46**
Hangleton. *W Sus* 2C **45**
Hankham. *E Sus* 2A **48**
Hannington. *Hants* 3B **22**
Hanscombe End. *Beds* 1D **7**
Hanwell. *G Lon* 3D **17**
Hanwell. *Oxon* 1A **4**
Hanworth. *G Lon* 1D **25**
Harbledown. *Kent* 3B **30**
Hardham. *W Sus* 1C **45**
Hardley. *Hants* 2A **42**
Hardway. *Hants* 2C **43**
Hardwick. *Buck* 3A **6**
Hardwick. *Oxon* 2B **4** (nr. Bicester)
Hardwick. *Oxon* 1A **14** (nr. Witney)
Hardy's Green. *Essx* 2D **11**
Harefield. *G Lon* 2C **17**
Hare Green. *Essx* 2A **12**
Hare Hatch. *Wok* 1A **24**
Hareplain. *Kent* 2C **39**
Hare Street. *Essx* 1C **19**
Hare Street. *Herts* 2B **8**
Harkstead. *Suff* 1B **12**
Harlington. *Beds* 1C **7**
Harlington. *G Lon* 1C **25**
Harlow. *Essx* 3C **9**
Harmer Green. *Herts* 3A **8**
Harmondsworth. *G Lon* 1C **25**
Harold Hill. *G Lon* 2D **19**
Harold Wood. *G Lon* 2D **19**
Harpenden. *Herts* 3D **7**
Harpsden. *Oxon* 3D **15**
Harrietsham. *Kent* 3C **29**
Harrow. *G Lon* 3D **17**
Harrow on the Hill. *G Lon* 3D **17**
Harrow Weald. *G Lon* 2D **17**
Hartfield. *E Sus* 2C **37**
Hartfordbridge. *Hants* 3D **23**
Hartford End. *Essx* 3A **10**
Hartley. *Kent* 2B **38** (nr. Cranbrook)
Hartley. *Kent* 2A **28** (nr. Dartford)
Hartley Mauditt. *Hants* 2D **33**
Hartley Wespall. *Hants* 3C **23**
Hartley Wintney. *Hants* 3D **23**
Hartlip. *Kent* 2C **29**
Harvel. *Kent* 2A **28**
Harwell. *Oxon* 3A **14**
Harwich. *Essx* 1C **13**
Hascombe. *Surr* 2B **34**
Haslemere. *Surr* 2B **34**
Hassell Street. *Kent* 1A **40**
Hassocks. *W Sus* 1B **46**
Haste Hill. *Surr* 2B **34**
Hastingleigh. *Kent* 1A **40**
Hastings. *E Sus* 2C **49**
Hastingwood. *Essx* 1C **19**
Hastoe. *Herts* 1B **16**
Hatch End. *G Lon* 2D **17**
Hatching Green. *Herts* 3D **7**
Hatch Warren. *Hants* 1C **33**
Hatfield. *Herts* 1A **18**
Hatfield Broad Oak. *Essx* 3D **9**
Hatfield Heath. *Essx* 3D **9**
Hatfield Hyde. *Herts* 3A **8**
Hatfield Peverel. *Essx* 3B **10**
Hatherden. *Hants* 3A **22**
Hattingley. *Hants* 2C **33**
Hatton. *G Lon* 1C **25**
Haultwick. *Herts* 2B **8**
Havant. *Hants* 2D **43**
Havenstreet. *IOW* 3B **42**
Haven, The. *W Sus* 2C **35**
Havering-atte-Bower. *G Lon* 2D **19**
Havering's Grove. *Essx* 2A **20**
Haversham. *Mil* 1A **6**
Hawkenbury. *Kent* 1C **39**
Hawkhurst. *Kent* 2B **38**
Hawkhurst Common. *E Sus* 1D **47**
Hawkinge. *Kent* 1C **41**
Hawkley. *Hants* 3D **33**
Hawkwell. *Essx* 2C **21**
Hawley. *Hants* 3A **24**
Hawley. *Kent* 1D **27**
Hawthorn Hill. *Brac* 1A **24**
Hayes. *G Lon* 2C **27** (nr. Bromley)
Hayes. *G Lon* 3C **17** (nr. Uxbridge)
Haylands. *IOW* 3B **42**
Hayling Island. *Hants* 3D **43**
Haynes. *Beds* 1C **7**
Haynes West End. *Beds* 1C **7**
Haysden. *Kent* 1D **37**
Hay Street. *Herts* 2B **8**
Haywards Heath. *W Sus* 3B **36**
Hazeleigh. *Essx* 1C **21**
Hazeley. *Hants* 3D **23**
Hazel Street. *Kent* 2A **38**
Hazlemere. *Buck* 2A **16**
Headbourne Worthy. *Hants* 2A **32**
Headcorn. *Kent* 1C **39**
Headington. *Oxon* 1B **14**
Headley. *Hants* 2A **34** (nr. Haslemere)
Headley. *Hants* 2B **22** (nr. Kingsclere)
Headley. *Surr* 3A **26**
Headley Down. *Hants* 2A **34**
Heath and Reach. *Beds* 2B **6**
Heath Common. *W Sus* 1D **45**
Heath End. *Hants* 2B **22**
Heathfield. *E Sus* 3D **37**
Heathrow (London) Airport. *G Lon* 1C **25**
Heathton. *Suff* 1B **12**
Heaverham. *Kent* 3D **27**
Hebing End. *Herts* 2B **8**
Heckfield. *Hants* 2D **23**
Heckfordbridge. *Essx* 2D **11**
Hedge End. *Hants* 1A **42**
Hedgerley. *Buck* 3B **16**

54 South East England Regional Road Atlas

Helions Bumpstead. *Essx* 1A **10**
Hellingly. *E Sus* 1D **47**
Helmdon. *Nptn* 1B **4**
Hemel Hempstead. *Herts* 1C **17**
Hemley. *Suff* 1C **13**
Hemp's Green. *Essx* 2D **11**
Hempstead. *Essx* 1A **10**
Hempstead. *Medw* 2B **28**
Hempton. *Oxon* 1A **4**
Hendon. *G Lon* 3A **18**
Henfield. *W Sus* 1A **46**
Henham. *Essx* 2D **9**
Henley. *W Sus* 3A **34**
Henley-on-Thames. *Oxon* 3D **15**
Henley's Down. *E Sus* 1B **48**
Henley Street. *Kent* 2A **28**
Henlow. *Beds* 1D **7**
Henny Street. *Essx* 1C **11**
Hensting. *Hants* 3A **32**
Henton. *Oxon* 1D **15**
Hermitage. *W Ber* 1B **22**
Hermitage. *W Sus* 2D **43**
Herne. *Kent* 2B **30**
Herne Bay. *Kent* 2B **30**
Herne Common. *Kent* 2B **30**
Herne Pound. *Kent* 3A **28**
Hernhill. *Kent* 2A **30**
Heronden. *Kent* 3C **31**
Herongate. *Essx* 2A **20**
Heronsgate. *Herts* 2C **17**
Heron's Ghyll. *E Sus* 3C **37**
Herriard. *Hants* 1C **33**
Hersden. *Kent* 2C **31**
Hersham. *Surr* 2D **25**
Herstmonceux. *E Sus* 1A **48**
Hertford. *Herts* 3B **8**
Hertford Heath. *Herts* 3B **8**
Hertingfordbury. *Herts* 3B **8**
Heston. *G Lon* 1D **25**
Hethe. *Oxon* 2B **4**
Hever. *Kent* 1C **37**
Hextable. *Kent* 1D **27**
Hexton. *Herts* 1D **7**
Heybridge. *Essx* 2A **20**
     (nr. Brentwood)
Heybridge. *Essx* 1C **21**
     (nr. Maldon)
Heybridge Basin. *Essx* 1C **21**
Heydon. *Cambs* 1C **9**
Heyshott. *W Sus* 1A **44**
Heythrop. *Oxon* 2A **4**
Hickstead. *W Sus* 3A **36**
Higham. *Kent* 1B **28**
Higham. *Suff* 1A **12**
Higham Gobion. *Beds* 1D **7**
Higham Wood. *Kent* 1D **37**
High Barnet. *G Lon* 2A **18**
High Beech. *Essx* 2C **19**
Highbrook. *W Sus* 2B **36**
High Brooms. *Kent* 1D **37**
Highclere. *Hants* 2A **22**
High Cogges. *Oxon* 1A **14**
High Cross. *Hants* 3D **33**
High Cross. *Herts* 3B **8**
High Easter. *Essx* 3A **10**
High Garrett. *Essx* 2B **10**
Highgate. *G Lon* 3A **18**
High Halden. *Kent* 2C **39**
High Halstow. *Medw* 1B **28**
High Hurstwood. *E Sus* 3C **37**
High Laver. *Essx* 1D **19**
Highleigh. *W Sus* 3A **44**
Highmoor. *Oxon* 3D **15**
High Ongar. *Essx* 1D **19**
High Roding. *Essx* 3A **10**
High Salvington. *W Sus* 2D **45**
Highsted. *Kent* 2D **29**
Highstreet Green. *Essx* 1B **10**
Highstreet Green. *Surr* 2B **34**
High Wych. *Herts* 3C **9**
High Wycombe. *Buck* 2A **16**
Hildenborough. *Kent* 1D **37**
Hillborough. *Kent* 2C **31**
Hill Brow. *Hants* 3D **33**
Hillesden. *Buck* 2C **5**
Hill Green. *Essx* 1C **9**
Hillgreen. *W Ber* 1A **22**
Hill Head. *Hants* 2B **42**
Hillingdon. *G Lon* 3C **17**
Hillside. *Hants* 3D **23**
Hill Top. *Hants* 2A **42**
Hilsea. *Port* 2C **43**
Hiltingbury. *Hants* 3A **32**
Hindhead. *Surr* 2A **34**
Hintlesham. *Suff* 1A **12**
Hinton Ampner. *Hants* 3B **32**
Hinton-in-the-Hedges. *Nptn* . . . 1B **4**
Hinton Waldrist. *Oxon* 2A **14**
Hinxhill. *Kent* 1A **40**
Hinxworth. *Herts* 1A **8**
Hipley. *Hants* 1C **43**
Hitchin. *Herts* 2D **7**
Hoaden. *Kent* 3C **31**
Hoath. *Kent* 2C **31**
Hobbs Cross. *Essx* 2C **19**

Hockley. *Essx* 2C **21**
Hockliffe. *Beds* 2B **6**
Hoddesdon. *Herts* 1B **18**
Hodsoll Street. *Kent* 2A **28**
Hoe Gate. *Hants* 1C **43**
Hogben's Hill. *Kent* 3A **30**
Hoggeston. *Buck* 2A **6**
Holborn. *G Lon* 3B **18**
Holbrook. *Suff* 1B **12**
Holbury. *Hants* 2A **42**
Holder's Green. *Essx* 2A **10**
Hole Street. *W Sus* 1D **45**
Holland-on-Sea. *Essx* 3C **13**
Hollingbourne. *Kent* 3C **29**
Hollingbury. *Brig* 2B **46**
Hollingdon. *Buck* 2A **6**
Hollingrove. *E Sus* 3A **38**
Hollington. *E Sus* 1B **48**
Holmbury St Mary. *Surr* 1D **35**
Holmer Green. *Buck* 2B **16**
Holt End. *Hants* 2C **33**
Holton. *Oxon* 1C **15**
Holton St Mary. *Suff* 1A **12**
Holt Pound. *Hants* 1A **34**
Holtsmere End. *Herts* 3C **7**
Holtye. *E Sus* 2C **37**
Holwell. *Herts* 1D **7**
Holybourne. *Hants* 1D **33**
Holyfield. *Essx* 1B **18**
Holyport. *Wind* 1A **24**
Honey Hill. *Kent* 2B **30**
Honey Tye. *Suff* 1D **11**
Honeywick. *Beds* 2B **6**
Hooe. *E Sus* 2A **48**
Hooe Common. *E Sus* 1A **48**
Hook. *G Lon* 2D **25**
Hook. *Hants* 3D **23**
     (nr. Basingstoke)
Hook. *Hants* 1D **42**
     (nr. Fareham)
Hook Green. *Kent* 2A **38**
     (nr. Lamberhurst)
Hook Green. *Kent* 1A **28**
     (nr. Longfield)
Hook Green. *Kent* 2A **28**
     (nr. Meopham)
Hook Norton. *Oxon* 1A **4**
Hook's Cross. *Herts* 2A **8**
Hookwood. *Surr* 1A **36**
Hooley. *Surr* 3A **26**
Hoo St Werburgh. *Medw* 1B **28**
Hope's Green. *Essx* 3B **20**
Horam. *E Sus* 1D **47**
Horkesley Heath. *Essx* 2D **11**
Horley. *Oxon* 1A **4**
Horley. *Surr* 1A **36**
Hornchurch. *G Lon* 3D **19**
Horndean. *Hants* 1C **43**
Horndon on the Hill. *Thur* 3A **20**
Horne. *Surr* 1B **36**
Horns Corner. *Kent* 3B **38**
Hornsey. *G Lon* 3B **18**
Horsebridge. *Hants* 2A **32**
Horsell. *Surr* 3B **24**
Horsenden. *Buck* 1D **15**
Horsham. *W Sus* 2D **35**
Horsley Cross. *Essx* 2B **12**
Horsleycross Street. *Essx* 2B **12**
Horsmonden. *Kent* 1A **38**
Horspath. *Oxon* 1B **14**
Horsted Keynes. *W Sus* 3B **36**
Horton. *Buck* 3B **6**
Horton. *Wind* 1C **25**
Horton-cum-Studley. *Oxon* . . . 3B **4**
Horton Heath. *Hants* 1A **42**
Horton Kirby. *Kent* 2D **27**
Hothfield. *Kent* 1D **39**
Houghton. *W Sus* 1C **45**
Houghton Conquest. *Beds* 1C **7**
Houghton Green. *E Sus* 3D **39**
Houghton Regis. *Beds* 2C **7**
Hound. *Hants* 2A **42**
Hound Green. *Hants* 3D **23**
Hounslow. *G Lon* 1D **25**
Hove. *Brig* . . . . 2A **46** & **62**
Howe Green. *Essx* 1B **20**
     (nr. Chelmsford)
Howegreen. *Essx* 1C **21**
     (nr. Maldon)
How End. *Beds* 1C **7**
Howe Street. *Essx* 3A **10**
     (nr. Chelmsford)
Howe Street. *Essx* 1A **10**
     (nr. Finchingfield)
How Green. *Kent* 1C **37**
Howlett End. *Essx* 1D **9**
Howt Green. *Kent* 2C **29**
Hoyle. *W Sus* 1B **44**
Hucking. *Kent* 3C **29**
Hughenden Valley. *Buck* 2A **16**
Hulcott. *Buck* 3A **6**
Hullbridge. *Essx* 2C **21**
Hundred Acres. *Hants* 1B **42**
Hungerford Newtown. *W Ber* . . 1A **22**
Hunny Hill. *IOW* 3A **42**

Hunsdon. *Herts* 3C **9**
Hunston. *W Sus* 2A **44**
Hunters Forstal. *Kent* 2B **30**
Hunton. *Hants* 3A **32**
Hunton. *Kent* 1B **38**
Hunton Bridge. *Herts* 1C **17**
Hurley. *Wind* 3A **16**
Hursley. *Hants* 3A **32**
Hurst. *Wok* 1A **24**
Hurstbourne Priors. *Hants* 1A **32**
Hurstbourne Tarrant. *Hants* . . . 3A **22**
Hurst Green. *E Sus* 3B **38**
Hurst Green. *Essx* 3C **13**
Hurst Green. *Surr* 3B **26**
Hurstpierpoint. *W Sus* 1A **46**
Hurst Wickham. *W Sus* 1A **46**
Hurtmore. *Surr* 1B **34**
Husborne Crawley. *Beds* 1B **6**
Hutton. *Essx* 2A **20**
Hyde Heath. *Buck* 1B **16**
Hydestile. *Surr* 1B **34**
Hythe. *Hants* 2A **42**
Hythe. *Kent* 2B **40**
Hythe End. *Wind* 1C **25**

I

Ibstone. *Buck* 2D **15**
Ibthorpe. *Hants* 3A **22**
Ibworth. *Hants* 3B **22**
Ickenham. *G Lon* 3C **17**
Ickford. *Buck* 1C **15**
Ickham. *Kent* 3C **31**
Ickleford. *Herts* 1D **7**
Icklesham. *E Sus* 1C **49**
Ickleton. *Cambs* 1C **9**
Ide Hill. *Kent* 3C **27**
Iden. *E Sus* 3D **39**
Iden Green. *Kent* 2C **39**
     (nr. Benenden)
Iden Green. *Kent* 2B **38**
     (nr. Goudhurst)
Iffley. *Oxon* 1B **14**
Ifield. *W Sus* 2A **36**
Ifieldwood. *W Sus* 2A **36**
Ifold. *W Sus* 2C **35**
Iford. *E Sus* 2C **47**
Ightham. *Kent* 3D **27**
Ilford. *G Lon* 3C **19**
Ilmer. *Buck* 1D **15**
Ingatestone. *Essx* 2A **20**
Ingrave. *Essx* 2A **20**
Inkpen. *W Ber* 2A **22**
Inworth. *Essx* 3C **11**
Iping. *W Sus* 3A **34**
Ipsden. *Oxon* 3C **15**
Ipswich. *Suff* 1B **12**
Isfield. *E Sus* 1C **47**
Isle of Thanet. *Kent* 2D **31**
Isleworth. *G Lon* 1D **25**
Islington. *G Lon* 3B **18**
Islip. *Oxon* 3B **4**
Istead Rise. *Kent* 1A **28**
Itchen. *Sotn* 1A **42**
Itchen Abbas. *Hants* 2B **32**
Itchen Stoke. *Hants* 2B **32**
Itchingfield. *W Sus* 3D **35**
Iver Heath. *Buck* 3C **17**
Ivinghoe. *Buck* 3B **6**
Ivinghoe Aston. *Buck* 3B **6**
Ivychurch. *Kent* 3A **40**
Ivy Hatch. *Kent* 3D **27**
Iwade. *Kent* 2D **29**

J

Jacobswell. *Surr* 3B **24**
Jarvis Brook. *E Sus* 3D **37**
Jasper's Green. *Essx* 2B **10**
Jaywick. *Essx* 3B **12**
Jevington. *E Sus* 2D **47**
Jockey End. *Herts* 3C **7**
John's Cross. *E Sus* 3B **38**
Jordans. *Buck* 2B **16**
Jury's Gap. *E Sus* 1D **49**

K

Kearsney. *Kent* 1C **41**
Kelshall. *Herts* 1B **8**
Kelvedon. *Essx* 3C **11**
Kelvedon Hatch. *Essx* 2D **19**
Kempshott. *Hants* 3C **23**
Kemp Town. *Brig* 2B **46**
Kemsing. *Kent* 3D **27**
Kemsley. *Kent* 2D **29**
Kenardington. *Kent* 2D **39**
Kenley. *G Lon* 3B **26**
Kennington. *Kent* 1A **40**
Kennington. *Oxon* 1B **14**
Kensington. *G Lon* 1A **26**
Kensworth. *Beds* 3C **7**

Kensworth Common. *Beds* 3C **7**
Kent International (Manston) Airport.
     Kent 2D **31**
Kenton. *G Lon* 3D **17**
Kent Street. *E Sus* 1B **48**
Kent Street. *Kent* 3A **28**
Kent Street. *W Sus* 3A **36**
Keston. *G Lon* 2C **27**
Kew. *G Lon* 1D **25**
Keymer. *W Sus* 1B **46**
Key Street. *Kent* 2C **29**
Kidbrooke. *G Lon* 1C **27**
Kiddington. *Oxon* 2A **4**
Kidlington. *Oxon* 3A **4**
Kidmore End. *Oxon* 1C **23**
Kilburn. *G Lon* 3A **18**
Killinghurst. *Surr* 2B **34**
Kilmeston. *Hants* 3B **32**
Kilndown. *Kent* 2B **38**
Kiln Green. *Wind* 1A **24**
Kimble Wick. *Buck* 1A **16**
Kimpton. *Herts* 3D **7**
Kingsash. *Buck* 1A **16**
Kingsbury. *G Lon* 3D **17**
Kingsclere. *Hants* 3B **22**
Kingsdown. *Kent* 1D **41**
Kingsey. *Buck* 1D **15**
Kingsfold. *W Sus* 2D **35**
Kingsgate. *Kent* 1D **31**
Kings Hill. *Kent* 3A **28**
Kings Langley. *Herts* 1C **17**
Kingsley. *Hants* 2D **33**
Kingsley Green. *W Sus* 2A **34**
Kingsnorth. *Kent* 2A **40**
Kingsnorth. *Medw* 1C **29**
King's Somborne. *Hants* 2A **32**
King's Sutton. *Nptn* 1A **4**
Kingston. *Kent* 3B **30**
Kingston. *W Sus* 2C **45**
Kingston Bagpuize. *Oxon* 2A **14**
Kingston Blount. *Oxon* 2D **15**
Kingston by Sea. *W Sus* 2A **46**
Kingston near Lewes. *E Sus* . . . 2B **46**
Kingston Stert. *Oxon* 1D **15**
Kingston upon Thames. *G Lon* . . 2D **25**
King's Walden. *Herts* 2D **7**
Kingswood. *Buck* 3C **5**
Kingswood. *Kent* 3C **29**
Kingswood. *Surr* 3A **26**
Kings Worthy. *Hants* 2A **32**
Kinsbourne Green. *Herts* 3D **7**
Kintbury. *W Ber* 2A **22**
Kipping's Cross. *Kent* 1A **38**
Kirby Cross. *Essx* 2C **13**
Kirby-le-Soken. *Essx* 2C **13**
Kirdford. *W Sus* 3C **35**
Kirtlington. *Oxon* 3B **4**
Kirton. *Suff* 1C **13**
Kite Hill. *IOW* 3B **42**
Kitwood. *Hants* 2C **33**
Knaphill. *Surr* 3B **24**
Knapp. *Hants* 3A **32**
Knatts Valley. *Kent* 2D **27**
Knebworth. *Herts* 2A **8**
Knockholt. *Kent* 3C **27**
Knockholt Pound. *Kent* 3C **27**
Knotty Green. *Buck* 2B **16**
Knowle Village. *Hants* 2B **42**
Knowl Hill. *Wind* 1A **24**
Knowlton. *Kent* 3C **31**

L

Lacey Green. *Buck* 1A **16**
Laddingford. *Kent* 1A **38**
Lagness. *W Sus* 2A **44**
Laindon. *Essx* 3A **20**
Laleham. *Surr* 2C **25**
Lamarsh. *Essx* 1C **11**
Lamb Corner. *Essx* 1A **12**
Lamberhurst. *Kent* 2A **38**
Lamberhurst Quarter. *Kent* . . . 2A **38**
Lambeth. *G Lon* 1B **26**
Lambourne End. *Essx* 2C **19**
Lambs Green. *W Sus* 2A **36**
Lancing. *W Sus* 2D **45**
Landport. *Port* 2C **43**
Lane End. *Buck* 2A **16**
Lane End. *Hants* 3B **32**
Lane End. *IOW* 3C **43**
Langdon Hills. *Essx* 3A **20**
Langdown. *Hants* 2A **42**
Langenhoe. *Essx* 3A **12**
Langford. *Beds* 1D **7**
Langford. *Essx* 1C **21**
Langham. *Essx* 1A **12**
Langley. *Essx* 1C **9**
Langley. *Hants* 2A **42**
Langley. *Herts* 2A **8**
Langley. *Kent* 3C **29**
Langley. *Slo* 1C **25**
Langley. *W Sus* 3A **34**
Langleybury. *Herts* 1C **17**
Langley Green. *W Sus* 2A **36**

Langley Heath. *Kent* 3C **29**
Langney. *E Sus* 2A **48**
Langrish. *Hants* 3D **33**
Langstone. *Hants* 2D **43**
Langton Green. *Kent* 2D **37**
Larkfield. *Kent* 3A **28**
Lasham. *Hants* 1C **33**
Lashenden. *Kent* 1C **39**
Latchford. *Herts* 2B **8**
Latchford. *Oxon* 1C **15**
Latchingdon. *Essx* 1C **21**
Latchmere Green. *Hants* 2C **23**
Latimer. *Buck* 2C **17**
Laughton. *E Sus* 1D **47**
Launton. *Oxon* 2C **5**
Laverstoke. *Hants* 1A **32**
Lawford. *Essx* 1A **12**
Layer Breton. *Essx* 3D **11**
Layer-de-la-Haye. *Essx* 2D **11**
Layer Marney. *Essx* 3D **11**
Layland's Green. *W Ber* 2A **22**
Layter's Green. *Buck* 2B **16**
Leaden Roding. *Essx* 3D **9**
Leadingcross Green. *Kent* 3C **29**
Leagrave. *Lutn* 2C **7**
Leatherhead. *Surr* 3D **25**
Leaveland. *Kent* 3A **30**
Leavenheath. *Suff* 1D **11**
Leaves Green. *G Lon* 2C **27**
Leckford. *Hants* 2A **32**
Leckhampstead. *Buck* 1D **5**
Leckhampstead. *W Ber* 1A **22**
Leckhampstead Street. *W Ber* . . 1A **22**
Ledburn. *Buck* 2B **6**
Ledwell. *Oxon* 2A **4**
Lee. *G Lon* 1C **27**
Lee. *Hants* 1A **42**
Lee Clump. *Buck* 1B **16**
Leeds. *Kent* 3C **29**
Lee-on-the-Solent. *Hants* 2B **42**
Lees, The. *Kent* 3A **30**
Lee, The. *Buck* 1B **16**
Leigh. *Kent* 1D **37**
Leigh. *Surr* 1A **36**
Leigh Beck. *Essx* 3C **21**
Leigh Green. *Kent* 2D **39**
Leigh-on-Sea. *S'end* 3C **21**
Leigh Park. *Hants* 2D **43**
Leighton Buzzard. *Beds* 2B **6**
Lemsford. *Herts* 3A **8**
Lenham. *Kent* 3C **29**
Lenham Heath. *Kent* 1D **39**
Lepe. *Hants* 3A **42**
Letchmore Heath. *Herts* 2D **17**
Letchworth Garden City. *Herts* . . . 1A **8**
Letcombe Bassett. *Oxon* 3A **14**
Letcombe Regis. *Oxon* 3A **14**
Letty Green. *Herts* 3A **8**
Levens Green. *Herts* 2B **8**
Levington. *Suff* 1C **13**
Lewes. *E Sus* 1C **47**
Lewisham. *G Lon* 1B **26**
Lewknor. *Oxon* 2D **15**
Lewson Street. *Kent* 2D **29**
Leybourne. *Kent* 3A **28**
Ley Green. *Herts* 2D **7**
Ley Hill. *Buck* 1B **16**
Leysdown-on-Sea. *Kent* 1A **30**
Leyton. *G Lon* 3B **18**
Leytonstone. *G Lon* 3C **19**
Lickfold. *W Sus* 3B **34**
Lidham Hill. *E Sus* 1C **49**
Lidlington. *Beds* 1B **6**
Lidsey. *W Sus* 2B **44**
Lidstone. *Oxon* 2A **4**
Lightwater. *Surr* 2B **24**
Lilley. *Herts* 2D **7**
Lillingstone Dayrell. *Buck* 1D **5**
Lillingstone Lovell. *Buck* 1D **5**
Limbury. *Lutn* 2C **7**
Limpsfield. *Surr* 3B **26**
Linchmere. *W Sus* 2A **34**
Lindfield. *W Sus* 3B **36**
Lindford. *Hants* 2A **34**
Lindsell. *Essx* 2A **10**
Linford. *Thur* 1A **28**
Lingfield. *Surr* 1B **36**
Linkenholt. *Hants* 3A **22**
Linslade. *Beds* 2B **6**
Linton. *Kent* 3B **28**
Liphook. *Hants* 2A **34**
Lisle Court. *Hants* 3A **42**
Liss. *Hants* 3D **33**
Liss Forest. *Hants* 3D **33**
Litchfield. *Hants* 3A **22**
Litlington. *Cambs* 1B **8**
Litlington. *E Sus* 2D **47**
Little Baddow. *Essx* 1B **20**
Little Bardfield. *Essx* 1A **10**
Little Bentley. *Essx* 2B **12**
Little Berkhamsted. *Herts* 1A **18**
Little Billington. *Beds* 2B **6**
Little Bognor. *W Sus* 3C **35**
Little Bookham. *Surr* 3D **25**
Littlebourne. *Kent* 3C **31**

Little Brickhill. *Mil* 1B **6**
Little Bromley. *Essx* 2A **12**
Little Burstead. *Essx* 2A **20**
Littlebury. *Essx* 1D **9**
Littlebury Green. *Essx* 1C **9**
Little Canfield. *Essx* 2D **9**
Little Chalfont. *Buck* 2B **16**
Little Chart. *Kent* 1D **39**
Little Chesterford. *Essx* 1D **9**
Little Chishill. *Cambs* 1C **9**
Little Clacton. *Essx* 3B **12**
Little Common. *E Sus* 2B **48**
Little Cornard. *Suff* 1C **11**
Littlecote. *Buck* 2A **6**
Little Down. *Hants* 3A **22**
Little Dunmow. *Essx* 2A **10**
Little Easton. *Essx* 2A **10**
Little End. *Essx* 1D **19**
Little Gaddesden. *Herts* 3B **6**
Little Hadham. *Herts* 2C **9**
Little Hallingbury. *Essx* 3C **9**
Little Hampden. *Buck* 1A **16**
Little Haseley. *Oxon* 1C **15**
Little Horkesley. *Essx* 1D **11**
Little Hormead. *Herts* 2C **9**
Little Horsted. *E Sus* 1C **47**
Little Horwood. *Buck* 1D **5**
Little Kimble. *Buck* 1A **16**
Little Kingshill. *Buck* 2A **16**
Little Laver. *Essx* 1D **19**
Little Leighs. *Essx* 3B **10**
Little London. *Buck* 3C **5**
Little London. *E Sus* 1D **47**
Little London. *Hants* 1A **32**
(nr. Andover)
Little London. *Hants* 3C **23**
(nr. Basingstoke)
Little Maplestead. *Essx* 1C **11**
Little Marlow. *Buck* 3A **16**
Little Milton. *Oxon* 1C **15**
Little Missenden. *Buck* 2B **16**
Littlemore. *Oxon* 1B **14**
Little Oakley. *Essx* 2C **13**
Little Posbrook. *Hants* 2B **42**
Little Sampford. *Essx* 1A **10**
Little Sandhurst. *Brac* 2A **24**
Little Somborne. *Hants* 3A **32**
Littlestone-on-Sea. *Kent* 3A **40**
Little Tew. *Oxon* 2A **4**
Little Tey. *Essx* 2C **11**
Little Thurrock. *Thur* 1A **28**
Littleton. *Hants* 2A **32**
Littleton. *Surr* 1B **34**
(nr. Guildford)
Littleton. *Surr* 2C **25**
(nr. Staines)
Little Totham. *Essx* 3C **11**
Little Wakering. *Essx* 3D **21**
Little Walden. *Essx* 1D **9**
Little Waltham. *Essx* 3B **10**
Little Warley. *Essx* 2A **20**
Little Wenham. *Suff* 1A **12**
Littlewick Green. *Wind* 1A **24**
Little Wittenham. *Oxon* 2B **14**
Littleworth. *W Sus* 3D **35**
Little Wymondley. *Herts* 2A **8**
Little Yeldham. *Essx* 1B **10**
Littley Green. *Essx* 3A **10**
Litton. *Somset* . . . . (missing)
Liverton. *Surr* (missing)
Lockscreen. *IOW* 3A **42**
Locks Heath. *Hants* 2B **42**
Lodsworth. *W Sus* 3B **34**
London. *G Lon* . . . . . . 3B **18** & 64-65
London Ashford (Lydd) Airport.
 Kent 3A **40**
London Biggin Hill Airport. *G Lon* . . 2C **27**
London City Airport. *G Lon* 3C **19**
London Colney. *Herts* 1D **17**
London Gatwick Airport. *W Sus* . . 1A **36**
London Heathrow Airport. *G Lon* . . 1C **25**
London Luton Airport. *Lutn* 2D **7**
London Southend Airport. *Essx* . . 3C **21**
London Stansted Airport. *Essx* . . 2D **9**
Long Common. *Hants* 1B **42**
Long Crendon. *Buck* 1C **15**
Longcross. *Surr* 2B **24**
Long Ditton. *Surr* 2D **25**
Longfield. *Kent* 2A **28**
Longfield Hill. *Kent* 2A **28**
Longford. *G Lon* 1C **25**
Long Gardens. *Essx* 1C **11**
Long Hanborough. *Oxon* 3A **4**
Longlane. *W Ber* 1A **22**
Long Marston. *Herts* 3A **6**
Longmoor Camp. *Hants* 2D **33**
Longparish. *Hants* 1A **32**
Longstock. *Hants* 2A **32**
Long Sutton. *Hants* 1D **33**
Longwick. *Buck* 1D **15**
Long Wittenham. *Oxon* 2B **14**
Longworth. *Oxon* 1A **14**
Loose. *Kent* 3B **28**
Loosley Row. *Buck* 1A **16**
Lordington. *W Sus* 2D **43**
Loudwater. *Buck* 2B **16**

Loughton. *Essx* 2C **19**
Loughton. *Mil* 1A **6**
Lovedean. *Hants* 1C **43**
Loves Green. *Essx* 1A **20**
Lower Arncott. *Oxon* 3C **5**
Lower Assendon. *Oxon* 3D **15**
Lower Basildon. *W Ber* 1C **23**
Lower Beeding. *W Sus* 3A **36**
Lower Bordean. *Hants* 3C **33**
Lower Bullington. *Hants* 1A **32**
Lower Common. *Hants* 1A **32**
Lower Dicker. *E Sus* 1D **47**
Lower Farringdon. *Hants* 2D **33**
Lower Froyle. *Hants* 1D **33**
Lower Gravenhurst. *Beds* 1D **7**
Lower Green. *Essx* 1C **9**
Lower Green. *W Ber* 2A **22**
Lower Halstow. *Kent* 2C **29**
Lower Hardres. *Kent* 3B **30**
Lower Heyford. *Oxon* 2A **4**
Lower Higham. *Kent* 1B **28**
Lower Holbrook. *Suff* 1B **12**
Lower Horncroft. *W Sus* 1C **45**
Lower Horsebridge. *E Sus* 1D **47**
Lower Kingswood. *Surr* 3A **26**
Lower Layham. *Suff* 1A **12**
Lower Nazeing. *Essx* 1B **18**
Lower Rainham. *Medw* 2C **29**
Lower Raydon. *Suff* 1A **12**
Lower Shelton. *Beds* 1B **6**
Lower Shiplake. *Oxon* 1D **23**
Lower Stoke. *Medw* 1C **29**
Lower Sundon. *Beds* 2C **7**
Lower Swanwick. *Hants* 2A **42**
Lower Upham. *Hants* 1B **42**
Lower Upnor. *Medw* 1B **28**
Lower Wield. *Hants* 1C **33**
Lower Winchendon. *Buck* 3D **5**
Lower Woodend. *Buck* 3A **16**
Lowfield Heath. *W Sus* 1A **36**
Lowford. *Hants* 1A **42**
Loxhill. *Surr* 2C **35**
Loxwood. *W Sus* 2C **35**
Luddenham. *Kent* 2D **29**
Luddesdown. *Kent* 2A **28**
Ludgershall. *Buck* 3C **5**
Luffenhall. *Herts* 2A **8**
Lunsford. *Kent* 3B **28**
Lunsford's Cross. *E Sus* 1B **48**
Lurgashall. *W Sus* 3B **34**
Luton. *Lutn* 2C **7**
Luton (London) Airport. *Lutn* . . . 2D **7**
Lydd. *Kent* 3A **40**
Lydden. *Kent* 1C **41**
(nr. Dover)
Lydden. *Kent* 2D **31**
(nr. Margate)
Lydd (London Ashford) Airport.
 Kent 3A **40**
Lydd-on-Sea. *Kent* 3A **40**
Lyde Green. *Hants* 3D **23**
Lye Green. *Buck* 1B **16**
Lye Green. *E Sus* 2D **37**
Lyford. *Oxon* 1A **14**
Lymbridge Green. *Kent* 1B **40**
Lyminge. *Kent* 1B **40**
Lyminster. *W Sus* 2C **45**
Lympne. *Kent* 2B **40**
Lyne. *Surr* 2C **25**
Lynsted. *Kent* 2D **29**

M

Mackerye End. *Herts* 3D **7**
Madehurst. *W Sus* 1B **44**
Magdalen Laver. *Essx* 1D **19**
Magham Down. *E Sus* 1A **48**
Maidenbower. *W Sus* 2A **36**
Maidenhead. *Wind* 3A **16**
Maiden's Green. *Brac* 1A **24**
Maidensgrove. *Oxon* 3D **15**
Maids Moreton. *Buck* 1D **5**
Maidstone. *Kent* 3B **28**
Malden Rushett. *G Lon* 2D **25**
Maldon. *Essx* 1C **21**
Mallows Green. *Essx* 2C **9**
Maltman's Hill. *Kent* 1D **39**
Mannings Heath. *W Sus* 3A **36**
Manningtree. *Essx* 1B **12**
Manor Park. *G Lon* 3C **19**
Manston. *Kent* 2D **31**
Manuden. *Essx* 2C **9**
Maple Cross. *Herts* 2C **17**
Mapledurham. *Oxon* 1C **23**
Mapledurwell. *Hants* 3C **23**
Maplehurst. *W Sus* 3D **35**
Maplescombe. *Kent* 2D **27**
Marcham. *Oxon* 1A **14**
Marchwood. *Hants* 1A **42**
Marden. *Kent* 1B **38**
Marden Beech. *Kent* 1B **38**
Marden Thorn. *Kent* 1B **38**
Marehill. *W Sus* 1C **45**
Maresfield. *E Sus* 3C **37**

Margaret Roding. *Essx* 3D **9**
Margaretting. *Essx* 1A **20**
Margaretting Tye. *Essx* 1A **20**
Margate. *Kent* 1D **31**
Margery. *Surr* 3A **26**
Marine Town. *Kent* 1D **29**
Markbeech. *Kent* 1C **37**
Mark Cross. *E Sus* 2D **37**
Mark's Corner. *IOW* 3A **42**
Marks Tey. *Essx* 2D **11**
Markyate. *Herts* 3C **7**
Marle Green. *E Sus* 1D **47**
Marlow. *Buck* 3A **16**
Marlow Bottom. *Buck* 3A **16**
Marlpit Hill. *Kent* 1C **37**
Marlpits. *E Sus* 3C **37**
Marsh. *Buck* 1A **16**
Marshalswick. *Herts* 1D **17**
Marsh Baldon. *Oxon* 2B **14**
Marsh Benham. *W Ber* 2A **22**
Marshborough. *Kent* 3D **31**
Marsh Gibbon. *Buck* 2C **5**
Marsh Green. *Kent* 1C **37**
Marshside. *Kent* 2C **31**
Marston. *Oxon* 1B **14**
Marston Moretaine. *Beds* 1B **6**
Marston St Lawrence. *Nptn* 1B **4**
Marsworth. *Buck* 3B **6**
Martin. *Kent* 1D **41**
Martin Mill. *Kent* 1D **41**
Martyr's Green. *Surr* 3C **25**
Martyr Worthy. *Hants* 2B **32**
Marylebone. *G Lon* 3A **18**
Mashbury. *Essx* 3A **10**
Matching. *Essx* 3D **9**
Matching Green. *Essx* 3D **9**
Matching Tye. *Essx* 3D **9**
Matfield. *Kent* 1A **38**
Mattingley. *Hants* 3D **23**
Maulden. *Beds* 1C **7**
Maxton. *Kent* 1C **41**
Maybush. *Sotn* 1A **42**
Mayes Green. *Surr* 2D **35**
Mayfield. *E Sus* 3D **37**
Mayford. *Surr* 3B **24**
Mayland. *Essx* 1D **21**
Maylandsea. *Essx* 1D **21**
Maynard's Green. *E Sus* 1D **47**
Maypole. *Kent* 2C **31**
Meadle. *Buck* 1A **16**
Meath Green. *Surr* 1A **36**
Medmenham. *Buck* 3A **16**
Medstead. *Hants* 2C **33**
Medway Towns. *Medw* . . 2B **28** & **66**
Meesden. *Herts* 1C **9**
Mentmore. *Buck* 3B **6**
Meon. *Hants* 2B **42**
Meonstoke. *Hants* 3C **33**
Meopham. *Kent* 2A **28**
Meopham Green. *Kent* 2A **28**
Meopham Station. *Kent* 2A **28**
Meppershall. *Beds* 1D **7**
Mereworth. *Kent* 3A **28**
Merrow. *Surr* 3C **25**
Mersham. *Kent* 2A **40**
Merstham. *Surr* 3A **26**
Merston. *W Sus* 2A **44**
Merton. *G Lon* 1A **26**
Merton. *Oxon* 3B **4**
Messing. *Essx* 3C **11**
Micheldever. *Hants* 2B **32**
Micheldever Station. *Hants* 1B **32**
Michelmersh. *Hants* 3A **32**
Micklefield Green. *Herts* 2C **17**
Mickleham. *Surr* 3D **25**
Middle Assendon. *Oxon* 3D **15**
Middle Aston. *Oxon* 2A **4**
Middle Barton. *Oxon* 2A **4**
Middle Claydon. *Buck* 2D **5**
Middleton. *Essx* 1C **11**
Middleton. *Hants* 1A **32**
Middleton Cheney. *Nptn* 1B **4**
Middleton-on-Sea. *W Sus* 2B **44**
Middleton Stoney. *Oxon* 2B **4**
Midgham. *W Ber* 2B **22**
Midhurst. *W Sus* 3A **34**
Mid Lavant. *W Sus* 2A **44**
Milcombe. *Oxon* 1A **4**
Milebush. *Kent* 1B **38**
Mile End. *Essx* 2D **11**
Mile Oak. *Brig* 2A **46**
Mile Town. *Kent* 1D **29**
Milford. *Surr* 1B **34**
Milland. *W Sus* 3A **34**
Millbridge. *Surr* 1A **34**
Millbrook. *Beds* 1C **7**
Mill End. *Buck* 3D **15**
Millbrook. *Sotn* 1A **42**
Mill End. *Herts* 1B **8**
Mill Green. *Essx* 1A **20**
Mill Green. *Herts* 1A **18**
Mill Green. *Suff* 1A **12**
Mill Hill. *G Lon* 2A **18**
Mill Lane. *Hants* 3D **23**
Millow. *Beds* 1A **8**

Milstead—Picket Piece

Milstead. *Kent* 3D **29**
Milton. *Oxon* 1A **4**
(nr. Banbury)
Milton. *Oxon* 2A **14**
(nr. Didcot)
Milton. *Port* 3C **43**
Milton Bryan. *Beds* 1B **6**
Milton Common. *Oxon* 1C **15**
Milton Hill. *Oxon* 2A **14**
Milton Keynes. *Mil* 1A **6** & **67**
Milton Keynes Village. *Mil* 1A **6**
Milton Regis. *Kent* 2C **29**
Milton Street. *E Sus* 2D **47**
Mimbridge. *Surr* 2B **24**
Minsted. *W Sus* 3A **34**
Minster. *Kent* 2D **31**
(nr. Ramsgate)
Minster. *Kent* 1D **29**
(nr. Sheerness)
Mistley. *Essx* 1B **12**
Mistley Heath. *Essx* 1B **12**
Mitcham. *G Lon* 2A **26**
Mixbury. *Oxon* 1C **5**
Molash. *Kent* 3A **30**
Molehill Green. *Essx* 2D **9**
Moneyrow Green. *Wind* 1A **24**
Monken Hadley. *G Lon* 2A **18**
Monk's Gate. *W Sus* 3A **36**
Monk Sherborne. *Hants* 3C **23**
Monks Risborough. *Buck* 1A **16**
Monk Street. *Essx* 2A **10**
Monkton. *Kent* 2C **31**
Monkwood. *Hants* 2C **33**
Moon's Green. *Kent* 3C **39**
Moorgreen. *Hants* 1A **42**
Moorhouse. *Surr* 3C **27**
Moor, The. *Kent* 3B **38**
Morden. *G Lon* 2A **26**
Morestead. *Hants* 3B **32**
Moreton. *Essx* 1D **19**
Moreton. *Oxon* 1C **15**
Morris Green. *Essx* 1B **10**
Mortimer Common. *W Ber* 2C **23**
Mortimer West End. *Hants* 2C **23**
Mottingham. *G Lon* 1C **27**
Mott's Mill. *E Sus* 2D **37**
Moulsecoomb. *Brig* 2B **46**
Moulsford. *Oxon* 3B **14**
Moulsoe. *Mil* 1B **6**
Mountain Street. *Kent* 3A **30**
Mount Bures. *Essx* 1D **11**
Mountfield. *E Sus* 3B **38**
Mountnessing. *Essx* 2A **20**
Mount Pleasant. *Buck* 1C **5**
Mount Pleasant. *E Sus* 1C **47**
Much Hadham. *Herts* 3C **9**
Mucking. *Thur* 3A **20**
Mugswell. *Surr* 3A **26**
Mundon. *Essx* 1C **21**
Murcott. *Oxon* 3B **4**
Murrell Green. *Hants* 3D **23**
Mursley. *Buck* 2A **6**
Muswell Hill. *G Lon* 3A **18**
Mytchett. *Surr* 3A **24**

N

Nackington. *Kent* 3B **30**
Nacton. *Suff* 1C **13**
Nalderswood. *Surr* 1A **36**
Naphill. *Buck* 2A **16**
Nash. *Buck* 1D **5**
Nash. *Kent* 3C **31**
Nash Lee. *Buck* 1A **16**
Nasty. *Herts* 2B **8**
Nately Scures. *Hants* 3D **23**
Navestock Heath. *Essx* 2D **19**
Navestock Side. *Essx* 2D **19**
Nayland. *Suff* 1D **11**
Nazeing. *Essx* 1C **19**
Neasden. *G Lon* 3A **18**
Neithrop. *Oxon* 1A **4**
Nethercott. *Oxon* 2A **4**
Netherfield. *E Sus* 1B **48**
Nether Street. *Essx* 3D **9**
Netherton. *Hants* 3A **22**
Nether Worton. *Oxon* 1A **4**
Netley. *Hants* 2A **42**
Nettlebed. *Oxon* 3D **15**
Nettleden. *Herts* 3C **7**
Nettlestead. *Kent* 3A **28**
Nettlestead Green. *Kent* 3A **28**
Nettlestone. *IOW* 3C **43**
Nevendon. *Essx* 2B **20**
New Addington. *G Lon* 2B **26**
New Alresford. *Hants* 2B **32**
New Ash Green. *Kent* 2A **28**
New Barn. *Kent* 2A **28**
Newbottle. *Nptn* 1B **4**
Newbourne. *Suff* 1C **13**
Newbridge. *IOW* 3A **42**
New Brighton. *Hants* 2D **43**
Newbury. *W Ber* 2A **22**
Newchapel. *Surr* 1B **36**
New Cheriton. *Hants* 3B **32**
Newchurch. *Kent* 2A **40**
New Denham. *Buck* 3C **17**
Newdigate. *Surr* 1D **35**
Newell Green. *Brac* 1A **24**
New Eltham. *G Lon* 1C **27**
Newenden. *Kent* 3C **39**
New England. *Essx* 1B **10**
Newfound. *Hants* 3B **22**
Newgate Street. *Herts* 1B **18**
New Greens. *Herts* 1D **17**
Newhaven. *E Sus* 2C **47**
New Haw. *Surr* 2C **25**
New Hythe. *Kent* 3B **28**
Newick. *E Sus* 3C **37**
Newington. *Kent* 2B **40**
(nr. Folkestone)
Newington. *Kent* 2C **29**
(nr. Sittingbourne)
Newington. *Oxon* 2C **15**
Newlands. *Essx* 3C **21**
New Malden. *G Lon* 2A **26**
Newman's Green. *Suff* 1C **11**
New Mill. *Herts* 3B **6**
New Mistley. *Essx* 1B **12**
Newnham. *Hants* 3D **23**
Newnham. *Herts* 1A **8**
Newnham. *Kent* 3D **29**
Newport. *Essx* 1D **9**
Newport. *IOW* 3B **42**
Newport Pagnell. *Mil* 1A **6**
Newpound Common. *W Sus* 3C **35**
New Romney. *Kent* 3A **40**
Newton. *Suff* 1D **11**
Newton Longville. *Buck* 1A **6**
Newton Purcell. *Oxon* 1C **5**
Newton Stacey. *Hants* 1A **32**
Newton Valence. *Hants* 2D **33**
Newtown. *Hants* 1B **42**
(nr. Bishop's Waltham)
Newtown. *Hants* 2A **22**
(nr. Newbury)
Newtown. *Hants* 2A **42**
(nr. Warsash)
Newtown. *Hants* 1C **43**
(nr. Wickham)
Newtown. *IOW* 3A **42**
New Town. *Lutn* 2C **7**
New Yatt. *Oxon* 3A **4**
Newyears Green. *G Lon* 3C **17**
Nine Ashes. *Essx* 1D **19**
Ninfield. *E Sus* 1B **48**
Ningwood. *IOW* 3A **42**
Noak Hill. *G Lon* 2D **19**
Noke. *Oxon* 3B **4**
Nonington. *Kent* 3C **31**
Norleywood. *Hants* 3A **42**
Normandy. *Surr* 3B **24**
Norman's Bay. *E Sus* 2A **48**
Northall. *Buck* 2B **6**
Northam. *Sotn* 1A **42**
North Ascot. *Brac* 2B **24**
North Aston. *Oxon* 2A **4**
Northaw. *Herts* 1A **18**
North Baddesley. *Hants* 3A **32**
North Benfleet. *Essx* 3B **20**
North Bersted. *W Sus* 2B **44**
North Boarhunt. *Hants* 1C **43**
Northbourne. *Kent* 3D **31**
Northbourne. *Oxon* 3B **14**
Northbrook. *Oxon* 2A **4**
North Chailey. *E Sus* 3B **36**
Northchapel. *W Sus* 3B **34**
Northchurch. *Herts* 1B **16**
North Common. *E Sus* 3B **36**
Northcourt. *Oxon* 2B **14**
North Cray. *G Lon* 1C **27**
Northend. *Buck* 2D **15**
North End. *Essx* 3A **10**
(nr. Great Dunmow)
North End. *Essx* 1B **10**
(nr. Great Yeldham)
North End. *Hants* 2A **22**
North End. *Port* 2C **43**
North End. *W Sus* 2D **45**
North Fambridge. *Essx* 2C **21**
Northfleet. *Kent* 1A **28**
North Halling. *Medw* 2B **28**
North Hayling. *Hants* 2D **43**
North Heath. *W Sus* 3C **35**
North Hinksey Village. *Oxon* 1A **14**
North Holmwood. *Surr* 1D **35**
Northiam. *E Sus* 3C **39**
Northington. *Hants* 2B **32**
North Lancing. *W Sus* 2D **45**
North Lee. *Buck* 1A **16**
North Leigh. *Kent* 1B **40**
North Leigh. *Oxon* 3A **4**
North Marden. *W Sus* 1A **44**
North Marston. *Buck* 2D **5**
Northmoor. *Oxon* 1A **14**
North Moreton. *Oxon* 3B **14**
North Mundham. *W Sus* 2A **44**
North Newington. *Oxon* 1A **4**
Northney. *Hants* 2D **43**
North Oakley. *Hants* 3B **22**
North Ockendon. *G Lon* 3D **19**
Northolt. *G Lon* 3D **17**
North Sheen. *G Lon* 1D **25**
North Shoebury. *S'end* 3D **21**
North Stifford. *Thur* 3A **20**
North Stoke. *Oxon* 3C **15**
North Stoke. *W Sus* 1C **45**
North Street. *Hants* 2C **33**
North Street. *Kent* 3A **30**
North Street. *Medw* 1C **29**
North Street. *W Ber* 1C **23**
North Waltham. *Hants* 1B **32**
North Warnborough. *Hants* 3D **23**
North Weald Bassett. *Essx* 1D **19**
North Weston. *Oxon* 1C **15**
Northwood. *G Lon* 2C **17**
Northwood. *IOW* 3A **42**
Northwood. *Kent* 2D **31**
Norton. *Herts* 1A **8**
Norton. *W Sus* 2B **44**
(nr. Arundel)
Norton. *W Sus* 3A **44**
(nr. Selsey)
Norton Green. *IOW* 3A **42**
Norton Heath. *Essx* 1A **20**
Norton Mandeville. *Essx* 1D **19**
Norwood Hill. *Surr* 1A **36**
Nounsley. *Essx* 3B **10**
Nuffield. *Oxon* 3C **15**
Nuneham Courtenay. *Oxon* 2B **14**
Nursling. *Hants* 1A **42**
Nursted. *W Sus* 3D **33**
Nutbourne. *W Sus* 2D **43**
(nr. Chichester)
Nutbourne. *W Sus* 1C **45**
(nr. Pulborough)
Nutfield. *Surr* 3B **26**
Nuthampstead. *Herts* 1C **9**
Nuthurst. *W Sus* 3D **35**
Nutley. *E Sus* 3C **37**
Nyetimber. *W Sus* 3A **44**
Nyewood. *W Sus* 3A **34**
Nyton. *W Sus* 2B **44**

O

Oad Street. *Kent* 2C **29**
Oakhanger. *Hants* 2D **33**
Oakley. *Buck* 3C **5**
Oakley. *Hants* 3B **22**
Oakley Green. *Wind* 1B **24**
Oakshott. *Hants* 3D **33**
Oakwoodhill. *Surr* 2D **35**
Oare. *Kent* 2A **30**
Oare. *W Ber* 1B **22**
Ockham. *Surr* 3C **25**
Ockley. *Surr* 1D **35**
Oddington. *Oxon* 3B **4**
Odiham. *Hants* 3D **23**
Odsey. *Cambs* 1A **8**
Offham. *E Sus* 1C **47**
Offham. *Kent* 3A **28**
Offham. *W Sus* 2C **45**
Offley Hoo. *Herts* 2D **7**
Old Alresford. *Hants* 2B **32**
Old Basing. *Hants* 3C **23**
Old Bexley. *G Lon* 1C **27**
Old Burghclere. *Hants* 3A **22**
Old Coulsdon. *G Lon* 3B **26**
Old Felixstowe. *Suff* 1D **13**
Old Grimsbury. *Oxon* 1A **4**
Old Heathfield. *E Sus* 3D **37**
Old Knebworth. *Herts* 2A **8**
Old Romney. *Kent* 3A **40**
Old Stratford. *Nptn* 1D **5**
Old Town. *E Sus* 3D **47**
Old Warden. *Beds* 1D **7**
Old Windsor. *Wind* 1B **24**
Old Wives Lees. *Kent* 3A **30**
Old Woking. *Surr* 3C **25**
Old Woodstock. *Oxon* 3A **4**
Oliver's Battery. *Hants* 3A **32**
Olmstead Green. *Cambs* 1A **10**
Onslow Green. *Essx* 3A **10**
Onslow Village. *Surr* 1B **34**
Ore. *E Sus* 1C **49**
Oreham Common. *W Sus* 1A **46**
Orlestone. *Kent* 2D **39**
Orpington. *G Lon* 2C **27**
Orsett. *Thur* 3A **20**
Ospringe. *Kent* 2A **30**
Ostend. *Essx* 2D **21**
Osterley. *G Lon* 1D **25**
Otford. *Kent* 3D **27**
Otham. *Kent* 3B **28**
Otterbourne. *Hants* 3A **32**
Otterham Quay. *Kent* 2C **29**
Ottershaw. *Surr* 2C **25**
Otterwood. *Hants* 2A **42**
Ottinge. *Kent* 1B **40**
Outwood. *Surr* 1B **36**
Over Kiddington. *Oxon* 2A **4**
Oversland. *Kent* 3A **30**
Overthorpe. *Nptn* 1A **4**
Overton. *Hants* 1B **32**
Over Worton. *Oxon* 2A **4**
Oving. *Buck* 2D **5**
Oving. *W Sus* 2B **44**
Ovingdean. *Brig* 2B **46**
Ovington. *Essx* 1B **10**
Ovington. *Hants* 2B **32**
Ower. *Hants* 2A **42**
Owlswick. *Buck* 1D **15**
Ownham. *W Ber* 1A **22**
Owslebury. *Hants* 3B **32**
Oxen End. *Essx* 2A **10**
Oxford. *Oxon* 1B **14** & **67**
Oxhey. *Herts* 2D **17**
Oxley Green. *Essx* 3D **11**
Oxley's Green. *E Sus* 3A **38**
Oxshott. *Surr* 2D **25**
Oxted. *Surr* 3B **26**

P

Pachesham. *Surr* 3D **25**
Padbury. *Buck* 1D **5**
Paddington. *G Lon* 3A **18**
Paddlesworth. *Kent* 2B **40**
Paddock. *Kent* 3D **29**
Paddock Wood. *Kent* 1A **38**
Padworth. *W Ber* 2C **23**
Pagham. *W Sus* 3A **44**
Paglesham Churchend. *Essx* 2D **21**
Paglesham Eastend. *Essx* 2D **21**
Paine's Corner. *E Sus* 3A **38**
Painter's Forstal. *Kent* 3D **29**
Palehouse Common. *E Sus* 1C **47**
Paley Street. *Wind* 1A **24**
Palmarsh. *Kent* 2B **40**
Pamber End. *Hants* 3C **23**
Pamber Green. *Hants* 3C **23**
Pamber Heath. *Hants* 2C **23**
Panfield. *Essx* 2B **10**
Pangbourne. *W Ber* 1C **23**
Paramour Street. *Kent* 2C **31**
Parbrook. *W Sus* 3C **35**
Pardown. *Hants* 1B **32**
Park Corner. *E Sus* 2D **37**
Park Corner. *Oxon* 3C **15**
Parkeston. *Essx* 1C **13**
Park Gate. *Hants* 2B **42**
Parkgate. *Surr* 1A **36**
Parkhurst. *IOW* 3A **42**
Park Street. *Herts* 1D **17**
Park Street. *W Sus* 2D **35**
Park Town. *Oxon* 1B **14**
Parmoor. *Buck* 3D **15**
Parsonage Green. *Essx* 3B **10**
Partridge Green. *W Sus* 1D **45**
Passenham. *Nptn* 1D **5**
Passfield. *Hants* 2A **34**
Passingford Bridge. *Essx* 2D **19**
Patcham. *Brig* 2B **46**
Patchetts Green. *Herts* 2D **17**
Patching. *W Sus* 2C **45**
Patmore Heath. *Herts* 2C **9**
Patrixbourne. *Kent* 3B **30**
Pattiswick. *Essx* 2C **11**
Peacehaven. *E Sus* 2C **47**
Peasemore. *W Ber* 1A **22**
Pease Pottage. *W Sus* 2A **36**
Peaslake. *Surr* 1C **35**
Peasmarsh. *E Sus* 3C **39**
Peasmarsh. *Surr* 1B **34**
Pebmarsh. *Essx* 1C **11**
Peckham Bush. *Kent* 3A **28**
Pedlinge. *Kent* 2B **40**
Peel Common. *Hants* 2B **42**
Peening Quarter. *Kent* 3C **39**
Pegsdon. *Beds* 1D **7**
Peldon. *Essx* 3D **11**
Pembury. *Kent* 1A **38**
Penge. *G Lon* 1B **26**
Penhurst. *E Sus* 1A **48**
Penn. *Buck* 2B **16**
Penn Street. *Buck* 2B **16**
Penshurst. *Kent* 1D **37**
Peper Harow. *Surr* 1B **34**
Perry Green. *Essx* 2C **11**
Perry Green. *Herts* 3C **9**
Perry Street. *Kent* 1A **28**
Perrywood. *Kent* 3A **30**
Petersfield. *Hants* 3D **33**
Peter's Green. *Herts* 3D **7**
Petham. *Kent* 3B **30**
Pett. *E Sus* 1C **49**
Pett Bottom. *Kent* 3B **30**
Petteridge. *Kent* 1A **38**
Petts Wood. *G Lon* 2C **27**
Petworth. *W Sus* 3B **34**
Pevensey. *E Sus* 2A **48**
Pevensey Bay. *E Sus* 2A **48**
Pheasants Hill. *Buck* 3D **15**
Phoenix Green. *Hants* 3D **23**
Piccotts End. *Herts* 1C **17**
Picket Piece. *Hants* 1A **32**

Piddinghoe. *E Sus* 2C **47**
Piddington. *Buck* 2A **16**
Piddington. *Oxon* 3C **5**
Pilgrims Hatch. *Essx* 2D **19**
Piltdown. *E Sus* 3C **37**
Pinkneys Green. *Wind* 3A **16**
Pin Mill. *Suff* 1C **13**
Pinner. *G Lon* 3D **17**
Pirbright. *Surr* 3B **24**
Pirton. *Herts* 1D **7**
Pishill. *Oxon* 3D **15**
Pitchcott. *Buck* 2D **5**
Pitch Green. *Buck* 1D **15**
Pitch Place. *Surr* 3B **24**
Pitsea. *Essx* 3B **20**
Pitstone. *Buck* 3B **6**
Pitt. *Hants* 3A **32**
Pittswood. *Kent* 1A **38**
Plaistow. *W Sus* 2C **35**
Plastow Green. *Hants* 2B **22**
Platt. *Kent* 3A **28**
Platt's Heath. *Kent* 3C **29**
Platt, The. *E Sus* 2D **37**
Plaxtol. *Kent* 3A **28**
Playden. *E Sus* 3D **39**
Play Hatch. *Oxon* 1D **23**
Pledgdon Green. *Essx* 2D **9**
Pleshey. *Essx* 3A **10**
Pluckley. *Kent* 1D **39**
Plummers Plain. *W Sus* 3A **36**
Plumpton. *E Sus* 1B **46**
Plumpton Green. *E Sus* 1B **46**
Plumstead. *G Lon* 1C **27**
Poffley End. *Oxon* 3A **4**
Point Clear. *Essx* 3A **12**
Polegate. *E Sus* 2D **47**
Poling. *W Sus* 2C **45**
Poling Corner. *W Sus* 2C **45**
Pollicott. *Buck* 3D **5**
Polstead. *Suff* 1D **11**
Polstead Heath. *Suff* 1D **11**
Ponders End. *G Lon* 2B **18**
Pond Street. *Essx* 1C **9**
Pondtail. *Hants* 3A **24**
Ponts Green. *E Sus* 1A **48**
Pooksgreen. *Hants* 1A **42**
Pool Street. *Essx* 1B **10**
Pootings. *Kent* 1C **37**
Popeswood. *Brac* 2A **24**
Popham. *Hants* 1B **32**
Poplar. *G Lon* 3B **18**
Popley. *Hants* 3C **23**
Porchfield. *IOW* 3A **42**
Portchester. *Hants* 2C **43**
Portsea. *Port* 2C **43**
Portslade-by-Sea. *Brig* 2A **46**
Portsmouth. *Port* . . . . 3C **43 & 68**
Port Solent. *Port* 2C **43**
Portswood. *Sotn* 1A **42**
Postcombe. *Oxon* 2D **15**
Postling. *Kent* 2B **40**
Potsgrove. *Beds* 2B **6**
Potten End. *Herts* 1C **17**
Potters Bar. *Herts* 1A **18**
Potters Crouch. *Herts* 1D **17**
Potterspury. *Nptn* 1D **5**
Potter Street. *Essx* 1C **19**
Poundfield. *E Sus* 2D **37**
Poundgate. *E Sus* 3C **37**
Pound Green. *E Sus* 3D **37**
Pound Hill. *W Sus* 2A **36**
Poundon. *Buck* 2C **5**
Pound Street. *Hants* 2A **22**
Pounsley. *E Sus* 3D **37**
Poyle. *Slo* 1C **25**
Poynings. *W Sus* 1A **46**
Pratt's Bottom. *G Lon* 2C **27**
Preston. *Brig* 2B **46**
Preston. *Herts* 2D **7**
Preston. *Kent* 2C **31**
             (nr. Canterbury)
Preston. *Kent* 2A **30**
            (nr. Faversham)
Preston Bissett. *Buck* 2C **5**
Preston Candover. *Hants* 1C **33**
Prestwood. *Buck* 1A **16**
Priestwood. *Brac* 1A **24**
Priestwood. *Kent* 2A **28**
Princes Risborough. *Buck* 1A **16**
Prinsted. *W Sus* 2D **43**
Prittlewell. *S'end* 3C **21**
Privett. *Hants* 3C **33**
Puckeridge. *Herts* 2B **8**
Pulborough. *W Sus* 1C **45**
Pulloxhill. *Beds* 1C **7**
Punnett's Town. *E Sus* 3A **38**
Purbrook. *Hants* 2C **43**
Purfleet. *Thur* 1D **27**
Purleigh. *Essx* 1C **21**
Purley. *G Lon* 2B **26**
Purley on Thames. *W Ber* 1C **23**
Pusey. *Oxon* 2A **14**
Putney. *G Lon* 1A **26**
Puttenham. *Herts* 3A **6**
Puttenham. *Surr* 1B **34**

Puttock End. *Essx* 1C **11**
Puttock's End. *Essx* 3D **9**
Pyecombe. *W Sus* 1A **46**
Pye Corner. *Herts* 3C **9**
Pyrford. *Surr* 3C **25**
Pyrton. *Oxon* 2C **15**

Q

Quainton. *Buck* 2D **5**
Quarrendon. *Buck* 3A **6**
Queenborough. *Kent* 1D **29**
Queen Street. *Kent* 1A **38**
Quendon. *Essx* 1D **9**
Quick's Green. *W Ber* 1B **22**
Quidhampton. *Hants* 3B **22**

R

Rableyheath. *Herts* 3A **8**
Rackham. *W Sus* 1C **45**
Radclive. *Buck* 1C **5**
Radfall. *Kent* 2B **30**
Radlett. *Herts* 2D **17**
Radley. *Oxon* 2B **14**
Radnage. *Buck* 2D **15**
Radstone. *Nptn* 1B **4**
Radwell. *Herts* 1A **8**
Radwinter. *Essx* 1A **10**
Rainham. *G Lon* 3D **19**
Rainham. *Medw* 2C **29**
Rake. *W Sus* 3A **34**
Ram Lane. *Kent* 1D **39**
Ramsden. *Hants* 3D **33**
Ramsdell. *Hants* 3B **22**
Ramsden. *Oxon* 3A **4**
Ramsden Bellhouse. *Essx* 2B **20**
Ramsden Heath. *Essx* 2B **20**
Ramsey. *Essx* 1C **13**
Ramsey Island. *Essx* 1D **21**
Ramsgate. *Kent* 2D **31**
Ramsnest Common. *Surr* 2B **34**
Rank's Green. *Essx* 3B **10**
Ranmore Common. *Surr* 3D **25**
Ratton Village. *E Sus* 2D **47**
Rawreth. *Essx* 2B **20**
Raydon. *Suff* 1A **12**
Rayleigh. *Essx* 2C **21**
Rayne. *Essx* 2B **10**
Rayners Lane. *G Lon* 3D **17**
Reading. *Read* . . . . 1D **23 & 68**
Reading Street. *Kent* 2D **39**
Reculver. *Kent* 2C **31**
Redbourn. *Herts* 3D **7**
Redford. *W Sus* 3A **34**
Redhill. *Herts* 1A **8**
Redhill. *Surr* 3A **26**
Reed. *Herts* 1B **8**
Reed End. *Herts* 1B **8**
Reigate. *Surr* 3A **26**
Remenham. *Wok* 3D **15**
Remenham Hill. *Wok* 3D **15**
Rettendon. *Essx* 2B **20**
Rew Street. *IOW* 3A **42**
Rhodes Minnis. *Kent* 1B **40**
Richborough Port. *Kent* 2D **31**
Richings Park. *Buck* 1C **25**
Richmond. *G Lon* 1D **25**
Rickling. *Essx* 1C **9**
Rickling Green. *Essx* 2D **9**
Rickmansworth. *Herts* 2C **17**
Ridge. *Herts* 1A **18**
Ridgewell. *Essx* 1B **10**
Ridgewood. *E Sus* 3C **37**
Ridgmont. *Beds* 1B **6**
Ridley. *Kent* 2A **28**
Ringlestone. *Kent* 3C **29**
Ringmer. *E Sus* 1C **47**
Ringshall. *Buck* 3B **6**
Ringwould. *Kent* 1D **41**
Ripe. *E Sus* 1D **47**
Ripley. *Surr* 3C **25**
Riplington. *Hants* 3C **33**
Ripple. *Kent* 1D **41**
Riseden. *E Sus* 3A **38**
Riseden. *Kent* 2B **38**
Riseley. *Wok* 2D **23**
Rivenhall. *Essx* 3C **11**
Rivenhall End. *Essx* 3C **11**
River. *Kent* 1D **41**
River. *W Sus* 3B **34**
Riverhead. *Kent* 3D **27**
Robertsbridge. *E Sus* 3B **38**
Robinhood End. *Essx* 1B **10**
Rochester. *Medw* 2B **28**
Rochford. *Essx* 2C **21**
Rock. *W Sus* 1D **45**
Rockwell End. *Buck* 3D **15**
Rodmell. *E Sus* 2C **47**
Rodmersham. *Kent* 2D **29**
Rodmersham Green. *Kent* 2D **29**
Roe Green. *Herts* 1B **8**
Roehampton. *G Lon* 1A **26**

Roffey. *W Sus* 2D **35**
Rogate. *W Sus* 3A **34**
Roke. *Oxon* 2C **15**
Rokemarsh. *Oxon* 2C **15**
Rolvenden. *Kent* 2C **39**
Rolvenden Layne. *Kent* 2C **39**
Romford. *G Lon* 3D **19**
Romsey. *Hants* 3A **32**
Rookwood. *W Sus* 3D **43**
Ropley. *Hants* 2C **33**
Ropley Dean. *Hants* 2C **33**
Rose Green. *Essx* 2C **11**
Rose Hill. *E Sus* 1C **47**
Roser's Cross. *E Sus* 3D **37**
Rotherfield. *E Sus* 3D **37**
Rotherfield Greys. *Oxon* 3D **15**
Rotherfield Peppard. *Oxon* 3D **15**
Rotherwick. *Hants* 3D **23**
Rotten Row. *W Ber* 1B **22**
Rottingdean. *Brig* 2B **46**
Rough Common. *Kent* 3B **30**
Roundbush Green. *Essx* 3D **9**
Roundhurst Common. *W Sus* 2B **34**
Roundstreet Common.
   W Sus 3C **35**
Rousham. *Oxon* 2A **4**
Rout's Green. *Buck* 2C **15**
Row Ash. *Hants* 1B **42**
Row Green. *Essx* 2B **10**
Row Heath. *Essx* 3B **12**
Rowhedge. *Essx* 2A **12**
Rowland's Castle. *Hants* 1D **43**
Rowledge. *Surr* 1A **34**
Rowly. *Surr* 1C **35**
Rowner. *Hants* 2C **43**
Rownhams. *Hants* 1A **42**
Rowsham. *Buck* 3A **6**
Rowstock. *Oxon* 3A **14**
Row Town. *Surr* 2C **25**
Roxwell. *Essx* 1A **20**
Royal Tunbridge Wells. *Kent* 2D **37**
Roydon. *Essx* 3C **9**
Roydon Hamlet. *Essx* 1C **19**
Royston. *Herts* 1B **8**
Ruckinge. *Kent* 2A **40**
Rucklers Lane. *Herts* 1C **17**
Rudgwick. *W Sus* 2C **35**
Rudley Green. *Essx* 1C **21**
Ruislip. *G Lon* 3C **17**
Ruislip Common. *G Lon* 3C **17**
Runcton. *W Sus* 2A **44**
Runfold. *Surr* 1A **34**
Runwell. *Essx* 2B **20**
Ruscombe. *Wok* 1C **23**
Rushden. *Herts* 1B **8**
Rushenden. *Kent* 1D **29**
Rush Green. *Herts* 2A **8**
Rushlake Green. *E Sus* 1A **48**
Rushmoor. *Surr* 1A **34**
Rusper. *W Sus* 2A **36**
Russell's Water. *Oxon* 3D **15**
Russ Hill. *Surr* 1A **36**
Rusthall. *Kent* 2D **37**
Rustington. *W Sus* 2C **45**
Ryarsh. *Kent* 3A **28**
Ryde. *IOW* 3B **42**
Rye. *E Sus* 3D **39**
Rye Foreign. *E Sus* 3D **39**
Rye Harbour. *E Sus* 1D **49**

S

Sacombe. *Herts* 3B **8**
Saddlescombe. *W Sus* 1A **46**
Saffron Walden. *Essx* 1D **9**
St Albans. *Herts* 1D **17**
St Cross. *Hants* 3A **32**
St Gile's Hill. *Hants* 3A **32**
St Helens. *E Sus* 1C **49**
St Helens. *IOW* 3C **43**
Saint Hill. *W Sus* 2B **36**
St Ippolyts. *Herts* 2D **7**
St Lawrence. *Essx* 1D **21**
St Leonards. *Buck* 1B **16**
St Leonards. *E Sus* 2B **48**
St Margaret's. *Herts* 3C **7**
          (nr. Hemel Hempstead)
St Margarets. *Herts* 3B **8**
           (nr. Hoddesdon)
St Margaret's at Cliffe. *Kent* 1D **41**
St Mary Bourne. *Hants* 3A **22**
St Mary Cray. *G Lon* 2C **27**
St Mary Hoo. *Medw* 1C **29**
St Mary in the Marsh. *Kent* 3A **40**
St Mary's Bay. *Kent* 3A **40**
St Michaels. *Kent* 2C **39**
St Nicholas at Wade. *Kent* 2C **31**
St Osyth. *Essx* 3B **12**
St Osyth Heath. *Essx* 3B **12**
St Paul's Cray. *G Lon* 2C **27**
St Paul's Walden. *Herts* 2D **7**
St Peter's. *Kent* 2D **31**
Salcott. *Essx* 3D **11**

Salehurst. *E Sus* 3B **38**
Salford. *Beds* 1B **6**
Salfords. *Surr* 1A **36**
Saltdean. *Brig* 2B **46**
Saltwood. *Kent* 2B **40**
Sanderstead. *G Lon* 2B **26**
Sandford-on-Thames. *Oxon* 1B **14**
Sandford St Martin. *Oxon* 2A **4**
Sandgate. *Kent* 2B **40**
Sandhills. *Surr* 2B **34**
Sandhurst. *Brac* 2A **24**
Sandhurst. *Kent* 3B **38**
Sandhurst Cross. *Kent* 3B **38**
Sandling. *Kent* 3B **28**
Sandon. *Essx* 1B **20**
Sandon. *Herts* 1B **8**
Sandridge. *Herts* 3D **7**
Sands, The. *Surr* 1A **34**
Sandway. *Kent* 3C **29**
Sandwich. *Kent* 3D **31**
Sarisbury. *Hants* 2B **42**
Sarratt. *Herts* 2C **17**
Sarre. *Kent* 2C **31**
Satwell. *Oxon* 3D **15**
Saunderton. *Buck* 1D **15**
Saunderton Lee. *Buck* 2A **16**
Sawbridgeworth. *Herts* 3C **9**
Sayers Common. *W Sus* 1A **46**
Scayne's Hill. *W Sus* 3B **36**
School Green. *Essx* 1B **10**
Scotland End. *Oxon* 1A **4**
Seabrook. *Kent* 2B **40**
Seaford. *E Sus* 3C **47**
Seal. *Kent* 3D **27**
Seale. *Surr* 1A **34**
Seasalter. *Kent* 2A **30**
Seaview. *IOW* 3C **43**
Seawick. *Essx* 3B **12**
Sedlescombe. *E Sus* 1B **48**
Seer Green. *Buck* 2B **16**
Selborne. *Hants* 2D **33**
Selham. *W Sus* 3B **34**
Sellindge. *Kent* 2B **40**
Selling. *Kent* 3A **30**
Selmeston. *E Sus* 2D **47**
Selsdon. *G Lon* 2B **26**
Selsey. *W Sus* 3A **44**
Selsfield Common. *W Sus* 2B **36**
Selsted. *Kent* 1C **41**
Send. *Surr* 3C **25**
Send Marsh. *Surr* 3C **25**
Sennicotts. *W Sus* 2A **44**
Sevenoaks. *Kent* 3D **27**
Sevenoaks Weald. *Kent* 3D **27**
Sevington. *Kent* 1A **40**
Sewards End. *Essx* 1D **9**
Sewardstone. *Essx* 2B **18**
Sewell. *Beds* 2B **6**
Shabbington. *Buck* 1C **15**
Shackleford. *Surr* 1B **34**
Shadoxhurst. *Kent* 2D **39**
Shalden. *Hants* 1C **33**
Shalfleet. *IOW* 3A **42**
Shalford. *Essx* 2B **10**
Shalford. *Surr* 1C **35**
Shalford Green. *Essx* 2B **10**
Shalmsford Street. *Kent* 3A **30**
Shalstone. *Buck* 1C **5**
Shamley Green. *Surr* 1C **35**
Sharnal Street. *Medw* 1B **28**
Sharpenhoe. *Beds* 1C **7**
Sharpthorne. *W Sus* 2B **36**
Shaw. *W Ber* 2A **22**
Shawford. *Hants* 3A **32**
Shedfield. *Hants* 1B **42**
Sheering. *Essx* 3D **9**
Sheerness. *Kent* 1D **29**
Sheerwater. *Surr* 2C **25**
Sheet. *Hants* 3D **33**
Sheffield Bottom. *W Ber* 2C **23**
Sheffield Green. *E Sus* 3C **37**
Shefford. *Beds* 1D **7**
Shefford Woodlands. *W Ber* 1A **22**
Sheldwich. *Kent* 3A **30**
Sheldwich Lees. *Kent* 3A **30**
Shelley. *Suff* 1A **12**
Shellow Bowells. *Essx* 1A **20**
Shenfield. *Essx* 2A **20**
Shenington. *Oxon* 1A **4**
Shenley. *Herts* 1D **17**
Shenley Brook End. *Mil* 1A **6**
Shenleybury. *Herts* 1D **17**
Shenley Church End. *Mil* 1A **6**
Shephall. *Herts* 2A **8**
Shepherd's Bush. *G Lon* 3A **18**
Shepherd's Green. *Oxon* 3D **15**
Shepherdswell. *Kent* 1C **41**
Shepperton. *Surr* 2C **25**
Shepway. *Kent* 3B **28**
Sherborne St John. *Hants* 3C **23**
Shere. *Surr* 1C **35**
Sherfield on Loddon. *Hants* 3C **23**
Shermanbury. *W Sus* 1A **46**
Shide. *IOW* 3B **42**
Shillingford. *Oxon* 2B **14**

Shillington. *Beds* 1D **7**
Shinfield. *Wok* 2D **23**
Shingle Street. *Suff* 1D **13**
Shipbourne. *Kent* 3D **27**
Shiplake. *Oxon* 1D **23**
Shipley. *W Sus* 3D **35**
Shipley Bridge. *Surr* 1B **36**
Shippon. *Oxon* 2A **14**
Shipton. *Buck* 2D **5**
Shipton Green. *W Sus* 3A **44**
Shipton-on-Cherwell. *Oxon* 3A **4**
Shirburn. *Oxon* 2C **15**
Shirkoak. *Kent* 2D **39**
Shirley. *Sotn* 1A **42**
Shirrell Heath. *Hants* 1B **42**
Shoeburyness. *S'end* 3D **21**
Sholden. *Kent* 3D **31**
Sholing. *Sotn* 1A **42**
Shoreditch. *G Lon* 3B **18**
Shoreham. *Kent* 2D **27**
Shoreham Airport. *W Sus* 2A **46**
Shoreham-by-Sea. *W Sus* 2A **46**
Shorne. *Kent* 1A **28**
Shorne Ridgeway. *Kent* 1A **28**
Shortbridge. *E Sus* 3C **37**
Shortgate. *E Sus* 1C **47**
Shotgate. *Essx* 2B **20**
Shotley. *Suff* 1C **13**
Shotley Gate. *Suff* 1C **13**
Shottenden. *Kent* 3A **30**
Shottermill. *Surr* 2A **34**
Shreding Green. *Buck* 3C **17**
Shripney. *W Sus* 2B **44**
Shrub End. *Essx* 2D **11**
Shurlock Row. *Wind* 1A **24**
Shutford. *Oxon* 1A **4**
Sibertswold. *Kent* 1C **41**
Sibford Ferris. *Oxon* 1A **4**
Sibford Gower. *Oxon* 1A **4**
Sible Hedingham. *Essx* 1B **10**
Sidcup. *G Lon* 1C **27**
Sidlesham. *W Sus* 3A **44**
Sidley. *E Sus* 2B **48**
Sidlowbridge. *Surr* 1A **36**
Silchester. *Hants* 2C **23**
Silsoe. *Beds* 1C **7**
Silver End. *Essx* 3C **11**
Sindlesham. *Wok* 2D **23**
Singleborough. *Buck* 1D **5**
Singleton. *Kent* 1D **39**
Singleton. *W Sus* 1A **44**
Singlewell. *Kent* 1A **28**
Sinkhurst Green. *Kent* 1C **39**
Sipson. *G Lon* 1C **25**
Sissinghurst. *Kent* 2B **38**
Sittingbourne. *Kent* 2D **29**
Skirmett. *Buck* 2D **15**
Skittle Green. *Buck* 1D **15**
Skye Green. *Essx* 2C **11**
Slade End. *Oxon* 2B **14**
Slade Green. *G Lon* 1D **27**
Slade, The. *W Ber* 2B **22**
Slapton. *Buck* 2B **6**
Slaugham. *W Sus* 3A **36**
Sleaford. *Hants* 2A **34**
Slindon. *W Sus* 2B **44**
Slinfold. *W Sus* 2D **35**
Slip End. *Beds* 3C **7**
Slough. *Slo* 3B **16**
Slough Green. *W Sus* 3A **36**
Small Dole. *W Sus* 1A **46**
Smallfield. *Surr* 1B **36**
Small Hythe. *Kent* 2C **39**
Smannell. *Hants* 1A **32**
Smarden. *Kent* 1C **39**
Smarden Bell. *Kent* 1C **39**
Smart's Hill. *Kent* 1D **37**
Smeeth. *Kent* 2A **40**
Smith's Green. *Essx* 2D **9**
Smyth's Green. *Essx* 3D **11**
Snargate. *Kent* 3D **39**
Snave. *Kent* 3A **40**
Snodland. *Kent* 2A **28**
Soake. *Hants* 1C **43**
Soberton. *Hants* 1C **43**
Soberton Heath. *Hants* 1C **43**
Soldridge. *Hants* 2C **33**
Solent Breezes. *Hants* 2B **42**
Sole Street. *Kent* 1A **28**
(nr. Meopham)
Sole Street. *Kent* 1A **40**
(nr. Waltham)
Somerley. *W Sus* 3A **44**
Somerton. *Oxon* 2A **4**
Sompting. *W Sus* 2D **45**
Sonning. *Wok* 1D **23**
Sonning Common. *Oxon* 3D **15**
Soulbury. *Buck* 2A **6**
Souldern. *Oxon* 1B **4**
Southall. *G Lon* 1D **25**
South Ambersham. *W Sus* 3B **34**
Southampton. *Sotn* . . . . .1A **42** & **69**
Southampton International Airport.
Hants 1A **42**
South Ascot. *Wind* 2B **24**

South Baddesley. *Hants* 3A **42**
South Benfleet. *Essx* 3B **20**
South Bersted. *W Sus* 2B **44**
Southborough. *Kent* 1D **37**
Southbourne. *W Sus* 2D **43**
Southchurch. *S'end* 3D **21**
South Common. *E Sus* 1B **46**
Southcourt. *Buck* 3A **6**
South Darenth. *Kent* 2D **27**
Southease. *E Sus* 2C **47**
South End. *W Ber* 1B **22**
Southend (London) Airport. *Essx* . .3C **21**
Southend-on-Sea. *S'end* 3C **21**
Southernden. *Kent* 1C **39**
Southey Green. *Essx* 1B **10**
South Fambridge. *Essx* 2C **21**
South Fawley. *W Ber* 3A **14**
Southfleet. *Kent* 1A **28**
Southgate. *G Lon* 2B **18**
South Godstone. *Surr* 1B **36**
South Green. *Essx* 2A **20**
(nr. Billericay)
South Green. *Essx* 3A **12**
(nr. Colchester)
South Green. *Kent* 2C **29**
South Hanningfield. *Essx* 2B **20**
South Harting. *W Sus* 1D **43**
South Hayling. *Hants* 3D **43**
South Heath. *Buck* 1B **16**
South Heath. *Essx* 3B **12**
South Heighton. *E Sus* 2C **47**
South Hinksey. *Oxon* 1B **14**
South Holmwood. *Surr* 1D **35**
South Hornchurch. *G Lon* 3D **19**
Southill. *Beds* 1D **7**
Southington. *Hants* 1B **32**
South Lancing. *W Sus* 2D **45**
South Leigh. *Oxon* 1A **14**
South Malling. *E Sus* 1C **47**
South Mimms. *Herts* 1A **18**
Southminster. *Essx* 2D **21**
Southmoor. *Oxon* 2A **14**
South Moreton. *Oxon* 3B **14**
South Mundham. *W Sus* 2A **44**
South Newington. *Oxon* 1A **4**
South Norwood. *G Lon* 2B **26**
South Nutfield. *Surr* 1B **36**
South Ockendon. *Thur* 3D **19**
South Oxhey. *Herts* 2D **17**
Southrope. *Hants* 1C **33**
Southsea. *Port* 3C **43**
South Stifford. *Thur* 1D **27**
South Stoke. *Oxon* 3B **14**
South Stoke. *W Sus* 1C **45**
South Street. *E Sus* 1B **46**
South Street. *Kent* 3A **30**
(nr. Faversham)
South Street. *Kent* 2B **30**
(nr. Whitstable)
South Town. *Hants* 2C **33**
South Warnborough. *Hants* 1D **33**
Southwater. *W Sus* 3D **35**
Southwater Street. *W Sus* 3D **35**
South Weald. *Essx* 2D **19**
South Weston. *Oxon* 2D **15**
Southwick. *Hants* 2C **43**
Southwick. *W Sus* 2A **46**
South Wonston. *Hants* 2A **32**
South Woodham Ferrers. *Essx* . .2C **21**
Sparrow's Green. *E Sus* 2A **38**
Sparsholt. *Hants* 2A **32**
Sparsholt. *Oxon* 3A **14**
Spear Hill. *W Sus* 1D **45**
Speen. *Buck* 2A **16**
Speen. *W Ber* 2A **22**
Speldhurst. *Kent* 1D **37**
Spellbrook. *Herts* 3C **9**
Spelsbury. *Oxon* 2A **4**
Spencers Wood. *Wok* 2D **23**
Spithurst. *E Sus* 1C **47**
Spreakley. *Surr* 1A **34**
Spring Vale. *IOW* 3C **43**
Stadhampton. *Oxon* 2C **15**
Stagden Cross. *Essx* 3A **10**
Staines. *Surr* 1C **25**
Stakes. *Hants* 2C **43**
Stalisfield Green. *Kent* 3D **29**
Stambourne. *Essx* 1B **10**
Stanborough. *Herts* 3A **8**
Stanbridge. *Beds* 2B **6**
Standen. *Kent* 1C **39**
Standen Street. *Kent* 2C **39**
Standford. *Hants* 2A **34**
Standlake. *Oxon* 1A **14**
Standon. *Hants* 3A **32**
Standon. *Herts* 2B **8**
Standon Green End. *Herts* 3B **8**
Stanford. *Beds* 1D **7**
Stanford. *Kent* 2B **40**
Stanford Dingley. *W Ber* 1B **22**
Stanford in the Vale. *Oxon* 2A **14**
Stanford-le-Hope. *Thur* 3A **20**
Stanford Rivers. *Essx* 1D **19**
Stanmer. *Brig* 2B **46**
Stanmore. *G Lon* 2D **17**

Stanmore. *Hants* 3A **32**
Stanmore. *W Ber* 1A **22**
Stanstead Abbotts. *Herts* 3B **8**
Stansted. *Kent* 2A **28**
Stansted (London) Airport. *Essx* . .2D **9**
Stansted Mountfitchet. *Essx* 2D **9**
Stanton Harcourt. *Oxon* 1A **14**
Stanton St John. *Oxon* 1B **14**
Stanway. *Essx* 2D **11**
Stanwell. *Surr* 1C **25**
Stanwell Moor. *Surr* 1C **25**
Staple. *Kent* 3C **31**
Staplecross. *E Sus* 3B **38**
Staplefield. *W Sus* 3A **36**
Stapleford. *Herts* 3B **8**
Stapleford Abbotts. *Essx* 2D **19**
Stapleford Tawney. *Essx* 2D **19**
Staplehurst. *Kent* 1B **38**
Staplers. *IOW* 3B **42**
Starling's Green. *Essx* 1C **9**
Start Hill. *Essx* 2D **9**
Stebbing. *Essx* 2A **10**
Stebbing Green. *Essx* 2A **10**
Stedham. *W Sus* 3A **34**
Steel Cross. *E Sus* 2D **37**
Steep. *Hants* 3D **33**
Steeple. *Essx* 1D **21**
Steeple Aston. *Oxon* 2A **4**
Steeple Barton. *Oxon* 2A **4**
Steeple Bumpstead. *Essx* 1A **10**
Steeple Claydon. *Buck* 2C **5**
Steeple Morden. *Cambs* 1A **8**
Stelling Minnis. *Kent* 1B **40**
Stepney. *G Lon* 3B **18**
Steppingley. *Beds* 1C **7**
Stevenage. *Herts* 2A **8**
Steventon. *Hants* 1B **32**
Steventon. *Oxon* 2A **14**
Stevington End. *Cambs* 1A **10**
Stewartby. *Beds* 1C **7**
Stewkley. *Buck* 2A **6**
Stewkley Dean. *Buck* 2A **6**
Steyning. *W Sus* 1D **45**
Stickling Green. *Essx* 1C **9**
Stisted. *Essx* 2B **10**
Stock. *Essx* 2A **20**
Stockbridge. *Hants* 2A **32**
Stockbury. *Kent* 2C **29**
Stockcross. *W Ber* 2A **22**
Stocker's Head. *Kent* 3D **29**
Stocking Green. *Essx* 1D **9**
Stocking Pelham. *Herts* 2C **9**
Stocks, The. *Kent* 3D **39**
Stockstreet. *Essx* 2C **11**
Stodmarsh. *Kent* 2C **31**
Stoke. *Hants* 3A **22**
(nr. Andover)
Stoke. *Hants* 2D **43**
(nr. South Hayling)
Stoke. *Medw* 1C **29**
Stoke by Clare. *Suff* 1B **10**
Stoke-by-Nayland. *Suff* 1D **11**
Stoke Charity. *Hants* 2A **32**
Stoke D'Abernon. *Surr* 3D **25**
Stoke Hammond. *Buck* 2A **6**
Stoke Lyne. *Oxon* 2B **4**
Stoke Mandeville. *Buck* 3A **6**
Stokenchurch. *Buck* 2D **15**
Stoke Newington. *G Lon* 3B **18**
Stoke Poges. *Buck* 3B **16**
Stoke Row. *Oxon* 3C **15**
Stoke Talmage. *Oxon* 2C **15**
Stondon Massey. *Essx* 1D **19**
Stone. *Buck* 3D **5**
Stone. *Kent* 1D **27**
Stonebridge. *Surr* 1D **35**
Stone Cross. *E Sus* 2A **48**
Stone Cross. *Kent* 2D **37**
Stonegate. *E Sus* 3A **38**
Stone Hill. *Kent* 2A **40**
Stone in Oxney. *Kent* 3D **39**
Stoner Hill. *Hants* 3D **33**
Stonesfield. *Oxon* 3A **4**
Stones Green. *Essx* 2B **12**
Stone Street. *Kent* 3D **27**
Stone Street. *Suff* 1D **11**
Stoneyhills. *Essx* 2D **21**
Stonor. *Oxon* 3D **15**
Stony Stratford. *Mil* 1D **5**
Stopham. *W Sus* 1C **45**
Stopsley. *Lutn* 2D **7**
Storrington. *W Sus* 1C **45**
Stotfold. *Beds* 1A **8**
Stoughton. *Surr* 3B **24**
Stoughton. *W Sus* 1A **44**
Stow Maries. *Essx* 2C **21**
Stowting. *Kent* 1B **40**
Stratfield Mortimer. *W Ber* 2C **23**
Stratfield Saye. *Hants* 2C **23**
Stratfield Turgis. *Hants* 3C **23**
Stratford. *G Lon* 3B **18**
Stratford St Mary. *Suff* 1A **12**
Stratton Audley. *Oxon* 2C **5**
Streat. *E Sus* 1B **46**
Streatham. *G Lon* 1A **26**

Streatley. *Beds* 2C **7**
Streatley. *W Ber* 3B **14**
Street End. *Kent* 3B **30**
Street End. *W Sus* 3A **44**
Strethall. *Essx* 1C **9**
Strood. *Kent* 2C **39**
Strood. *Medw* 2B **28**
Strood Green. *Surr* 1A **36**
Strood Green. *W Sus* 3C **35**
(nr. Billingshurst)
Strood Green. *W Sus* 2D **35**
(nr. Horsham)
Stroud. *Hants* 3D **33**
Stroud Green. *Essx* 2C **21**
Stubbington. *Hants* 2B **42**
Stubb's Cross. *Kent* 2D **39**
Studham. *Beds* 3C **7**
Stunts Green. *E Sus* 1A **48**
Sturmer. *Essx* 1A **10**
Sturry. *Kent* 2B **30**
Stutton. *Suff* 1B **12**
Sudbury. *Suff* 1C **11**
Sulham. *W Ber* 1C **23**
Sulhamstead. *W Ber* 2C **23**
Sullington. *W Sus* 1C **45**
Summersdale. *W Sus* 2A **44**
Sunbury. *Surr* 2D **25**
Sundon Park. *Lutn* 2C **7**
Sundridge. *Kent* 3C **27**
Sunningdale. *Wind* 2B **24**
Sunninghill. *Wind* 2B **24**
Sunningwell. *Oxon* 1A **14**
Sunnymead. *Oxon* 1B **14**
Sunnyside. *W Sus* 2B **36**
Surbiton. *G Lon* 2D **25**
Surrex. *Essx* 2C **11**
Sutton. *Buck* 1C **25**
Sutton. *E Sus* 3C **47**
Sutton. *G Lon* 2A **26**
Sutton. *Kent* 1D **41**
Sutton. *Oxon* 1A **14**
Sutton. *W Sus* 1B **44**
Sutton Abinger. *Surr* 1D **35**
Sutton at Hone. *Kent* 2D **27**
Sutton Courtenay. *Oxon* 2B **14**
Sutton Green. *Surr* 3C **25**
Sutton Scotney. *Hants* 2A **32**
Sutton Valence. *Kent* 1C **39**
Swalcliffe. *Oxon* 1A **4**
Swalecliffe. *Kent* 2B **30**
Swallowfield. *Wok* 2D **23**
Swampton. *Hants* 3A **22**
Swanbourne. *Buck* 2A **6**
Swanley. *Kent* 2D **27**
Swanmore. *Hants* 1B **42**
Swanscombe. *Kent* 1D **27**
Swan Street. *Essx* 2C **11**
Swanton Street. *Kent* 3C **29**
Swanwick. *Hants* 2B **42**
Swarraton. *Hants* 2B **32**
Swaythling. *Sotn* 1A **42**
Swerford. *Oxon* 1A **4**
Swiftsden. *E Sus* 3B **38**
Swinford. *Oxon* 1A **14**
Swingfield Minnis. *Kent* 1C **41**
Swingfield Street. *Kent* 1C **41**
Sydenham. *G Lon* 1B **26**
Sydenham. *Oxon* 1D **15**
Sydmonton. *Hants* 3A **22**
Syresham. *Nptn* 1C **5**

T

Tackley. *Oxon* 2A **4**
Tadley. *Hants* 2C **23**
Tadmarton. *Oxon* 1A **4**
Tadworth. *Surr* 3A **26**
Takeley. *Essx* 2D **9**
Takeley Street. *Essx* 2D **9**
Tandridge. *Surr* 3B **26**
Tangmere. *W Sus* 2B **44**
Tankerton. *Kent* 2B **30**
Taplow. *Buck* 3B **16**
Tarpots. *Essx* 3B **20**
Tarring Neville. *E Sus* 2C **47**
Taston. *Oxon* 2A **4**
Tatling End. *Buck* 3C **17**
Tatsfield. *Surr* 3C **27**
Tattingstone. *Suff* 1B **12**
Tattingstone White Horse. *Suff* . .1B **12**
Taverners Green. *Essx* 3D **9**
Taylors Green. *Essx* 2B **6**
Teddington. *G Lon* 1D **25**
Telham. *E Sus* 1B **48**
Telscombe. *E Sus* 2C **47**
Telscombe Cliffs. *E Sus* 2B **46**
Temple Ewell. *Kent* 1C **41**
Templeton. *W Ber* 2A **22**
Tendring. *Essx* 2B **12**
Tendring Green. *Essx* 2B **12**
Tenterden. *Kent* 2C **39**
Terrick. *Buck* 1A **16**
Teston. *Kent* 3B **28**

Testwood. *Hants* ... 1A **42**
Tetsworth. *Oxon* ... 1C **15**
Tewin. *Herts* ... 3A **8**
Teynham. *Kent* ... 2D **29**
Teynham Street. *Kent* ... 2D **29**
Thakeham. *W Sus* ... 1D **45**
Thame. *Oxon* ... 1D **15**
Thames Ditton. *Surr* ... 2D **25**
Thames Haven. *Thur* ... 3B **20**
Thamesmead. *G Lon* ... 3C **19**
Thamesport. *Medw* ... 1C **29**
Thanington Without. *Kent* ... 3B **30**
Thatcham. *W Ber* ... 2B **22**
Thaxted. *Essx* ... 1A **10**
Theale. *W Ber* ... 1C **23**
Thenford. *Nptn* ... 1B **4**
Therfield. *Herts* ... 1B **8**
Theydon Bois. *Essx* ... 2C **19**
Thong. *Kent* ... 1A **28**
Thorington Street. *Suff* ... 1A **12**
Thorley. *Herts* ... 3C **9**
Thorley Street. *Herts* ... 3C **9**
Thorley Street. *IOW* ... 3A **42**
Thornborough. *Buck* ... 1D **5**
Thorncombe Street. *Surr* ... 1B **34**
Thornhill. *Sotn* ... 1A **42**
Thornton. *Buck* ... 1D **5**
Thornton Heath. *G Lon* ... 2B **26**
Thornwood Common. *Essx* ... 1C **19**
Thorpe. *Surr* ... 2C **25**
Thorpe Bay. *S'end* ... 3D **21**
Thorpe Common. *Suff* ... 1C **13**
Thorpe Green. *Essx* ... 2B **12**
Thorpe-le-Soken. *Essx* ... 2B **12**
Thorrington. *Essx* ... 2A **12**
Three Bridges. *W Sus* ... 2A **36**
Three Chimneys. *Kent* ... 2C **39**
Three Cups Corner. *E Sus* ... 3A **38**
Three Leg Cross. *E Sus* ... 2A **38**
Three Mile Cross. *Wok* ... 2D **23**
Three Oaks. *E Sus* ... 1C **49**
Throcking. *Herts* ... 1B **8**
Throwley. *Kent* ... 3D **29**
Throwley Forstal. *Kent* ... 3D **29**
Thrupp. *Oxon* ... 3A **4**
Thundersley. *Essx* ... 3B **20**
Thundridge. *Herts* ... 3B **8**
Thurnham. *Kent* ... 3C **29**
Thursley. *Surr* ... 2B **34**
Ticehurst. *E Sus* ... 2A **38**
Tichborne. *Hants* ... 2B **32**
Tiddington. *Oxon* ... 1C **15**
Tidebrook. *E Sus* ... 3A **38**
Tidmarsh. *W Ber* ... 1C **23**
Tilbury. *Thur* ... 1A **28**
Tilbury Green. *Essx* ... 1B **10**
Tilbury Juxta Clare. *Essx* ... 1B **10**
Tilehurst. *Read* ... 1C **23**
Tilford. *Surr* ... 1A **34**
Tilgate Forest Row. *W Sus* ... 2A **36**
Tillingham. *Essx* ... 1D **21**
Tillington. *W Sus* ... 3B **34**
Tilmanstone. *Kent* ... 3D **31**
Tilsworth. *Beds* ... 2B **6**
Timsbury. *Hants* ... 3A **32**
Tingewick. *Buck* ... 1C **5**
Tingrith. *Beds* ... 1C **7**
Tinsley Green. *W Sus* ... 2A **36**
Tiptree. *Essx* ... 3C **11**
Tiptree Heath. *Essx* ... 3C **11**
Tisman's Common. *W Sus* ... 2C **35**
Titchfield. *Hants* ... 2B **42**
Titsey. *Surr* ... 3C **27**
Toddington. *Beds* ... 2C **7**
Tokers Green. *Oxon* ... 1D **23**
Tollesbury. *Essx* ... 3D **11**
Tolleshunt D'Arcy. *Essx* ... 3D **11**
Tolleshunt Knights. *Essx* ... 3D **11**
Tolleshunt Major. *Essx* ... 3D **11**
Tolworth. *G Lon* ... 2D **25**
Tonbridge. *Kent* ... 1D **37**
Tongham. *Surr* ... 1A **34**
Tonwell. *Herts* ... 3B **8**
Toot Baldon. *Oxon* ... 1B **14**
Toot Hill. *Essx* ... 1D **19**
Toot Hill. *Hants* ... 1A **42**
Toppesfield. *Essx* ... 1B **10**
Tortington. *W Sus* ... 2C **45**
Tottenham. *G Lon* ... 2B **18**
Totteridge. *G Lon* ... 2A **18**
Totternhoe. *Beds* ... 2B **6**
Totton. *Hants* ... 1A **42**
Touchen-end. *Wind* ... 1A **24**
Tower Hill. *W Sus* ... 3D **35**
Towersey. *Oxon* ... 1D **15**
Town Littleworth. *E Sus* ... 1C **47**
Town Row. *E Sus* ... 2D **37**
Towns End. *Hants* ... 3B **22**
Townsend. *Herts* ... 1D **17**
Toy's Hill. *Kent* ... 3C **27**
Trash Green. *W Ber* ... 2C **23**
Treyford. *W Sus* ... 1A **44**
Trimley Lower Street. *Suff* ... 1C **13**
Trimley St Martin. *Suff* ... 1C **13**
Trimley St Mary. *Suff* ... 1C **13**

Tring. *Herts* ... 3B **6**
Trottiscliffe. *Kent* ... 2A **28**
Trotton. *W Sus* ... 3A **34**
Trowley Bottom. *Herts* ... 3C **7**
Trumps Green. *Surr* ... 2B **24**
Tubney. *Oxon* ... 2A **14**
Tudeley. *Kent* ... 1A **38**
Tuesley. *Surr* ... 1B **34**
Tufton. *Hants* ... 1A **32**
Tumbler's Green. *Essx* ... 2C **11**
Tunstall. *Kent* ... 2C **29**
Tunworth. *Hants* ... 1C **33**
Turgis Green. *Hants* ... 3C **23**
Turkey Island. *Hants* ... 1B **42**
Turners Hill. *W Sus* ... 2B **36**
Turnford. *Herts* ... 1B **18**
Turville. *Buck* ... 2D **15**
Turville Heath. *Buck* ... 2D **15**
Turweston. *Buck* ... 1C **5**
Tutts Clump. *W Ber* ... 1B **22**
Twickenham. *G Lon* ... 1D **25**
Twineham. *W Sus* ... 3A **36**
Twinstead. *Essx* ... 1C **11**
Twinstead Green. *Essx* ... 1C **11**
Twyford. *Buck* ... 2C **5**
Twyford. *Hants* ... 3A **32**
Twyford. *Wok* ... 1D **23**
Tye. *Hants* ... 2D **43**
Tye Green. *Essx* ... 2D **9**
  (nr. Bishop's Stortford)
Tye Green. *Essx* ... 2B **10**
  (nr. Braintree)
Tye Green. *Essx* ... 1D **9**
  (nr. Saffron Walden)
Tyler Hill. *Kent* ... 2B **30**
Tylers Green. *Buck* ... 2A **16**
Tyler's Green. *Essx* ... 1D **19**

U

Uckfield. *E Sus* ... 3C **37**
Udimore. *E Sus* ... 1C **49**
Ufton Nervet. *W Ber* ... 2C **23**
Ugley. *Essx* ... 2D **9**
Ugley Green. *Essx* ... 2D **9**
Ulcombe. *Kent* ... 1C **39**
Ulting. *Essx* ... 1C **21**
Underriver. *Kent* ... 3D **27**
Union Street. *E Sus* ... 2B **38**
Upchurch. *Kent* ... 2C **29**
Upham. *Hants* ... 3B **32**
Uplees. *Kent* ... 2D **29**
Up Marden. *W Sus* ... 1D **43**
Up Nately. *Hants* ... 3C **23**
Upper Arncott. *Oxon* ... 3C **5**
Upper Astrop. *Nptn* ... 1B **4**
Upper Basildon. *W Ber* ... 1B **22**
Upper Beeding. *W Sus* ... 1D **45**
Upper Bucklebury. *W Ber* ... 2B **22**
Upper Bullington. *Hants* ... 1A **32**
Upper Clatford. *Hants* ... 1A **32**
Upper Cokeham. *W Sus* ... 2D **45**
Upper Common. *Hants* ... 1C **33**
Upper Dicker. *E Sus* ... 2D **47**
Upper Dovercourt. *Essx* ... 1C **13**
Upper Dunsley. *Herts* ... 3B **6**
Upper Enham. *Hants* ... 1A **32**
Upper Farringdon. *Hants* ... 2D **33**
Upper Froyle. *Hants* ... 1D **33**
Upper Gravenhurst. *Beds* ... 1D **7**
Upper Green. *Essx* ... 1C **9**
Upper Green. *W Ber* ... 2D **21**
Upper Hale. *Surr* ... 1A **34**
Upper Halliford. *Surr* ... 2C **25**
Upper Halling. *Medw* ... 2A **28**
Upper Hardres Court. *Kent* ... 3B **30**
Upper Hartfield. *E Sus* ... 2C **37**
Upper Heyford. *Oxon* ... 2A **4**
Upper Horsebridge. *E Sus* ... 1D **47**
Upper Layham. *Suff* ... 1A **12**
Upper North Dean. *Buck* ... 2A **16**
Upper Norwood. *W Sus* ... 1B **44**
Upper Shelton. *Beds* ... 1B **6**
Upper Stondon. *Beds* ... 1D **7**
Upper Street. *Suff* ... 1B **12**
Upper Sundon. *Beds* ... 2C **7**
Upperton. *W Sus* ... 3B **34**
Upper Tooting. *G Lon* ... 1A **26**
Upper Upnor. *Medw* ... 1B **28**
Upper Weald. *Mil* ... 1A **6**
Upper Wellingham. *E Sus* ... 1C **47**
Upper Wield. *Hants* ... 2C **33**
Upper Winchendon. *Buck* ... 3D **5**
Upper Wootton. *Hants* ... 3B **22**
Upshire. *Essx* ... 1C **19**
Upstreet. *Kent* ... 2C **31**
Upton. *Buck* ... 3D **5**
Upton. *Hants* ... 3A **22**
  (nr. Andover)
Upton. *Hants* ... 1A **42**
  (nr. Southampton)

Upton. *IOW* ... 3B **42**
Upton. *Oxon* ... 3B **14**
Upton. *Slo* ... 1B **24**
Upton End. *Beds* ... 1D **7**
Upton Grey. *Hants* ... 1C **33**
Upwaltham. *W Sus* ... 1B **44**
Upwick Green. *Herts* ... 2C **9**
Uxbridge. *G Lon* ... 3C **17**

V

Valley End. *Surr* ... 2B **24**
Vange. *Essx* ... 3B **20**
Vernham Street. *Hants* ... 3A **22**
Vigo Village. *Kent* ... 2A **28**
Vinehall Street. *E Sus* ... 3B **38**
Vine's Cross. *E Sus* ... 1D **47**
Virginia Water. *Surr* ... 2B **24**

W

Waddesdon. *Buck* ... 3D **5**
Wadesmill. *Herts* ... 3B **8**
Wadhurst. *E Sus* ... 2A **38**
Wadwick. *Hants* ... 3A **22**
Wainscott. *Medw* ... 1B **28**
Wakes Colne. *Essx* ... 2C **11**
Walberton. *W Sus* ... 2B **44**
Walderslade. *Medw* ... 2B **28**
Walderton. *W Sus* ... 1D **43**
Waldron. *E Sus* ... 1D **47**
Walkern. *Herts* ... 2A **8**
Wallands Park. *E Sus* ... 1C **47**
Wallcrouch. *E Sus* ... 2A **38**
Wallend. *Medw* ... 1C **29**
Wallingford. *Oxon* ... 3C **15**
Wallington. *G Lon* ... 2A **26**
Wallington. *Hants* ... 2B **42**
Wallington. *Herts* ... 1A **8**
Walliswood. *Surr* ... 2D **35**
Walmer. *Kent* ... 3D **31**
Walsworth. *Herts* ... 1D **7**
Walter's Ash. *Buck* ... 2A **16**
Waltham. *Kent* ... 1B **40**
Waltham Abbey. *Essx* ... 1B **18**
Waltham Chase. *Hants* ... 1B **42**
Waltham Cross. *Herts* ... 1B **18**
Waltham St Lawrence.
  Wind ... 1A **24**
Waltham's Cross. *Essx* ... 1A **10**
Walthamstow. *G Lon* ... 3B **18**
Walton. *Mil* ... 1A **6**
Walton. *Suff* ... 1C **13**
Walton-on-Thames. *Surr* ... 2D **25**
Walton on the Hill. *Surr* ... 3A **26**
Walton-on-the-Naze. *Essx* ... 2C **13**
Wanborough. *Surr* ... 1B **34**
Wandsworth. *G Lon* ... 1A **26**
Wannock. *E Sus* ... 2D **47**
Wanshurst Green. *Kent* ... 1B **38**
Wanstead. *G Lon* ... 3C **19**
Wantage. *Oxon* ... 3A **14**
Warbleton. *E Sus* ... 1A **48**
Warblington. *Hants* ... 2D **43**
Warborough. *Oxon* ... 2B **14**
Warden. *Kent* ... 1A **30**
Wardhedges. *Beds* ... 1C **7**
Wardley. *W Sus* ... 3A **34**
Ware. *Herts* ... 3B **8**
Ware. *Kent* ... 2C **31**
Warehorne. *Kent* ... 2D **39**
Wareside. *Herts* ... 3B **8**
Warfield. *Brac* ... 1A **24**
Wargrave. *Wok* ... 1D **23**
Warkworth. *Nptn* ... 1A **4**
Warlingham. *Surr* ... 3B **26**
Warminghurst. *W Sus* ... 1D **45**
Warners End. *Herts* ... 1C **17**
Warnford. *Hants* ... 3C **33**
Warnham. *W Sus* ... 2D **35**
Warningcamp. *W Sus* ... 2C **45**
Warninglid. *W Sus* ... 3A **36**
Warren Corner. *Hants* ... 1A **34**
  (nr. Aldershot)
Warren Corner. *Hants* ... 3D **33**
  (nr. Petersfield)
Warren Row. *Wind* ... 3A **16**
Warren Street. *Kent* ... 3D **29**
Warsash. *Hants* ... 2A **42**
Wartling. *E Sus* ... 2A **48**
Warwick Wold. *Surr* ... 3B **26**
Washbrook. *Suff* ... 1B **12**
Washington. *W Sus* ... 1D **45**
Wasp Green. *Surr* ... 1B **36**
Waterbeach. *W Sus* ... 2A **44**
Water End. *Beds* ... 1C **7**
Water End. *Herts* ... 1A **18**
  (nr. Hatfield)
Water End. *Herts* ... 3C **7**
  (nr. Hemel Hempstead)
Waterford. *Herts* ... 3B **8**
Wateringbury. *Kent* ... 3A **28**

Waterlooville. *Hants* ... 2C **43**
Waterperry. *Oxon* ... 1C **15**
Watersfield. *W Sus* ... 1C **45**
Waterside. *Buck* ... 1B **16**
Waterstock. *Oxon* ... 1C **15**
Water Stratford. *Buck* ... 1C **5**
Watford. *Herts* ... 2C **17**
Watlington. *Oxon* ... 2C **15**
Watton at Stone. *Herts* ... 3A **8**
Wavendon. *Mil* ... 1B **6**
Waverley. *Surr* ... 1A **34**
Wealdstone. *G Lon* ... 3D **17**
Weedon. *Buck* ... 3A **6**
Weeke. *Hants* ... 2A **32**
Weeley. *Essx* ... 2B **12**
Weeley Heath. *Essx* ... 2B **12**
Welford. *W Ber* ... 1A **22**
Welham Green. *Herts* ... 1A **18**
Well. *Hants* ... 1D **33**
Well Hill. *Kent* ... 2C **27**
Wellhouse. *W Ber* ... 1B **22**
Welling. *G Lon* ... 1C **27**
Wellow. *IOW* ... 3A **42**
Wellpond Green. *Herts* ... 2C **9**
Welwyn. *Herts* ... 3A **8**
Welwyn Garden City. *Herts* ... 3A **8**
Wembley. *G Lon* ... 3D **17**
Wendens Ambo. *Essx* ... 1D **9**
Wendlebury. *Oxon* ... 3B **4**
Wendover. *Buck* ... 1A **16**
Wennington. *G Lon* ... 3D **19**
Wepham. *W Sus* ... 2C **45**
West Ashling. *W Sus* ... 2A **44**
Westbere. *Kent* ... 2B **30**
West Bergholt. *Essx* ... 2D **11**
West Blatchington. *Brig* ... 2A **46**
Westbourne. *W Sus* ... 2D **43**
West Brabourne. *Kent* ... 1A **40**
Westbrook. *Kent* ... 1D **31**
West Burton. *W Sus* ... 1C **45**
Westbury. *Buck* ... 1C **5**
West Byfleet. *Surr* ... 2C **25**
West Challow. *Oxon* ... 3A **14**
West Chiltington. *W Sus* ... 1C **45**
West Chiltington Common.
  W Sus ... 1C **45**
West Clandon. *Surr* ... 3C **25**
West Cliffe. *Kent* ... 1D **41**
Westcliffe-on-Sea. *S'end* ... 3C **21**
Westcott. *Buck* ... 3D **5**
Westcott. *Surr* ... 1D **35**
Westcott Barton. *Oxon* ... 2A **4**
Westdean. *E Sus* ... 3D **47**
West Dean. *W Sus* ... 1A **44**
West Drayton. *G Lon* ... 1C **25**
West End. *Hants* ... 3A **18**
West End. *Hants* ... 1A **42**
West End. *Herts* ... 1A **18**
West End. *Kent* ... 2B **30**
West End. *Surr* ... 2B **24**
West End. *Wind* ... 1A **24**
West End Green. *Hants* ... 2C **23**
Westenhanger. *Kent* ... 2B **40**
Westergate. *W Sus* ... 2B **44**
Westerham. *Kent* ... 3C **27**
Westerton. *W Sus* ... 2A **44**
West Farleigh. *Kent* ... 3B **28**
Westfield. *E Sus* ... 1C **49**
West Firle. *E Sus* ... 2C **47**
Westgate on Sea. *Kent* ... 1D **31**
West Ginge. *Oxon* ... 3A **14**
West Green. *Hants* ... 3D **23**
West Grinstead. *W Sus* ... 3D **35**
West Hagbourne. *Oxon* ... 3B **14**
Westham. *E Sus* ... 2A **48**
West Ham. *G Lon* ... 3B **18**
Westhampnett. *W Sus* ... 2A **44**
West Hanney. *Oxon* ... 2A **14**
West Hanningfield. *Essx* ... 2B **20**
West Heath. *W Sus* ... 3D **33**
West Heath. *Hants* ... 3B **22**
  (nr. Basingstoke)
West Heath. *Hants* ... 3A **24**
  (nr. Farnborough)
West Hendred. *Oxon* ... 3A **14**
West Hill. *W Sus* ... 2B **36**
West Hoathly. *W Sus* ... 2B **36**
West Horndon. *Essx* ... 3A **20**
West Horsley. *Surr* ... 3C **25**
West Hougham. *Kent* ... 1C **41**
Westhumble. *Surr* ... 3D **25**
West Hyde. *Herts* ... 2C **17**
West Hythe. *Kent* ... 2B **40**
West Ilsley. *W Ber* ... 3A **14**
West Itchenor. *W Sus* ... 2A **44**
West Kingsdown. *Kent* ... 2D **27**
West Langdon. *Kent* ... 1D **41**
West Lavington. *W Sus* ... 3A **34**
West Leith. *Buck* ... 3B **6**
Westlington. *Buck* ... 3D **5**
West Malling. *Kent* ... 3A **28**
West Marden. *W Sus* ... 1D **43**
Westmarsh. *Kent* ... 2C **31**
West Meon. *Hants* ... 3C **33**
West Mersea. *Essx* ... 3A **12**

Westmeston. *E Sus* 1B **46**
Westmill. *Herts* 2B **8**
  (nr. Buntingford)
Westmill. *Herts* 1D **7**
  (nr. Hitchin)
Westminster. *G Lon* 1A **26**
West Molesey. *Surr* 2D **25**
West Norwood. *G Lon* 1B **26**
Weston. *Hants* 3D **33**
Weston. *Herts* 1A **8**
Weston. *W Ber* 1A **22**
Westoning. *Beds* 1C **7**
Weston-on-the-Green. *Oxon* 3B **4**
Weston Patrick. *Hants* 1C **33**
Weston Turville. *Buck* 3A **6**
West Peckham. *Kent* 3A **28**
West Stoke. *W Sus* 2A **44**
West Stourmouth. *Kent* 2C **31**
West Stratton. *Hants* 1B **32**
West Street. *Kent* 3D **29**
West Thorney. *W Sus* 2D **43**
West Thurrock. *Thur* 1D **27**
West Tilbury. *Thur* 1A **28**
West Tisted. *Hants* 3C **33**
West Town. *Hants* 3D **43**
Westwell. *Kent* 1D **39**
Westwell Leacon. *Kent* 1D **39**
West Wickham. *G Lon* 2B **26**
West Wittering. *W Sus* 3D **43**
Westwood. *Kent* 2D **31**
West Woodhay. *W Ber* 2A **22**
West Worldham. *Hants* 2D **33**
West Worthing. *W Sus* 2D **45**
West Wycombe. *Buck* 2A **16**
Wethersfield. *Essx* 1B **10**
Wexham Street. *Buck* 3B **16**
Weybourne. *Surr* 1A **34**
Weybridge. *Surr* 2C **25**
Whaddon. *Buck* 1A **6**
Wharley End. *Beds* 1B **6**
Whatlington. *E Sus* 1B **48**
Wheathampstead. *Herts* 3D **7**
Wheatley. *Hants* 1D **33**
Wheatley. *Oxon* 1B **14**
Wheelerstreet. *Surr* 1B **34**
Whelpley Hill. *Buck* 1B **16**
Wherstead. *Suff* 1B **12**
Wherwell. *Hants* 1A **32**
Whetsted. *Kent* 1A **38**
Whetstone. *G Lon* 2A **18**
Whippingham. *IOW* 3B **42**
Whipsnade. *Beds* 3C **7**
Whistley Green. *Wok* 1D **23**
Whitchurch. *Buck* 2A **6**
Whitchurch. *Hants* 1A **32**
Whitchurch Hill. *Oxon* 1C **23**
Whitchurch-on-Thames. *Oxon* 1C **23**
Whiteash Green. *Essx* 1B **10**
White Colne. *Essx* 2C **11**
Whitehall. *Hants* 3D **23**
Whitehall. *W Sus* 3D **35**
Whitehill. *Hants* 2D **33**
Whiteley. *Hants* 2B **42**
Whiteley Village. *Surr* 2C **25**
Whitemans Green. *W Sus* 3B **36**
Whitenap. *Hants* 3A **32**
White Notley. *Essx* 3B **10**
Whiteoak Green. *Oxon* 3A **4**
White Roding. *Essx* 3D **9**
Whitesmith. *E Sus* 1D **47**
Whitestreet Green. *Suff* 1D **11**

White Waltham. *Wind* 1A **24**
Whitfield. *Kent* 1D **41**
Whitfield. *Nptn* 1C **5**
Whitstable. *Kent* 2B **30**
Whitway. *Hants* 3A **22**
Whitwell. *Herts* 2D **7**
Whyteleafe. *Surr* 3B **26**
Wichling. *Kent* 3D **29**
Wick. *W Sus* 2C **45**
Wicken. *Nptn* 1D **5**
Wicken Bonhunt. *Essx* 1C **9**
Wicker Street Green. *Suff* 1D **11**
Wickford. *Essx* 2B **20**
Wickham. *Hants* 1B **42**
Wickham. *W Ber* 1A **22**
Wickham Bishops. *Essx* 3C **11**
Wickhambreaux. *Kent* 3C **31**
Wickham Heath. *W Ber* 2A **22**
Wickham St Paul. *Essx* 1C **11**
Wick Hill. *Wok* 2D **23**
Widdington. *Essx* 1D **9**
Widford. *Essx* 1A **20**
Widford. *Herts* 3C **9**
Widmer End. *Buck* 2A **16**
Wiggens Green. *Essx* 1A **10**
Wigginton. *Herts* 3B **6**
Wigginton. *Oxon* 1A **4**
Wiggonholt. *W Sus* 1C **45**
Wigmore. *Medw* 2C **29**
Wildern. *Hants* 1A **42**
Wildhern. *Hants* 3A **22**
Willen. *Mil* 1A **6**
Willesborough. *Kent* 1A **40**
Willesborough Lees. *Kent* 1A **40**
Willesden. *G Lon* 3A **18**
Willey Green. *Surr* 3B **24**
Willian. *Herts* 1A **8**
Willingale. *Essx* 1D **19**
Willingdon. *E Sus* 2D **47**
Willows Green. *Essx* 3B **10**
Wilmington. *E Sus* 2D **47**
Wilmington. *Kent* 1D **27**
Wilsley Green. *Kent* 2B **38**
Wilstead. *Beds* 1C **7**
Wilstone. *Herts* 3B **6**
Wimbish. *Essx* 1D **9**
Wimbish Green. *Essx* 1A **10**
Wimbledon. *G Lon* 1A **26**
Winchelsea. *E Sus* 1D **49**
Winchelsea Beach. *E Sus* 1D **49**
Winchester. *Hants* . . . . . 3A **32 & 69**
Winchet Hill. *Kent* 1B **38**
Winchfield. *Hants* 3D **23**
Winchmore Hill. *Buck* 2B **16**
Winchmore Hill. *G Lon* 2B **18**
Windlesham. *Surr* 2B **24**
Windmill Hill. *E Sus* 1A **48**
Windsor. *Wind* . . . . 1B **24 & 69**
Wineham. *W Sus* 3A **36**
Wing. *Buck* 2A **6**
Wingfield. *Beds* 2C **7**
Wingham. *Kent* 3C **31**
Wingmore. *Kent* 1B **40**
Wingrave. *Buck* 3A **6**
Winkfield. *Brac* 1B **24**
Winkfield Row. *Brac* 1A **24**
Winklebury. *Hants* 3C **23**
Winnersh. *Wok* 1D **23**
Winslade. *Hants* 1C **33**
Winslow. *Buck* 2D **5**
Winterbourne. *W Ber* 1A **22**

Winterbrook. *Oxon* 3C **15**
Winter Gardens. *Essx* 3B **20**
Winton. *E Sus* 2D **47**
Wisborough Green. *W Sus* 3C **35**
Wisley. *Surr* 3C **25**
Wissenden. *Kent* 1D **39**
Wiston. *W Sus* 1D **45**
Witham. *Essx* 3C **11**
Witherenden Hill. *E Sus* 3A **38**
Witheridge Hill. *Oxon* 3C **15**
Withermarsh Green. *Suff* 1A **12**
Withyham. *E Sus* 2C **37**
Witley. *Surr* 1B **34**
Witney. *Oxon* 3A **4**
Wittersham. *Kent* 3D **39**
Wivelrod. *Hants* 2C **33**
Wivelsfield. *E Sus* 3B **36**
Wivelsfield Green. *E Sus* 1B **46**
Wivenhoe. *Essx* 2A **12**
Wix. *Essx* 2B **12**
Wixoe. *Suff* 1B **10**
Woburn. *Beds* 1B **6**
Woburn Sands. *Mil* 1B **6**
Woking. *Surr* 3C **25**
Wokingham. *Wok* 2A **24**
Woldingham. *Surr* 3B **26**
Wolvercote. *Oxon* 1A **14**
Wolverton. *Hants* 3B **22**
Wolverton. *Mil* 1A **6**
Wolverton Common. *Hants* 3B **22**
Womenswold. *Kent* 3C **31**
Wonersh. *Surr* 1C **35**
Wonston. *Hants* 2A **32**
Wooburn. *Buck* 3B **16**
Wooburn Green. *Buck* 3B **16**
Woodchurch. *Kent* 2D **39**
Woodcote. *Oxon* 3C **15**
Woodcott. *Hants* 3A **22**
Woodeaton. *Oxon* 3B **4**
Wood End. *Herts* 2B **8**
Woodend. *W Sus* 2A **44**
Woodend Green. *Essx* 2D **9**
Woodford. *G Lon* 2B **18**
Woodford Green. *G Lon* 2C **19**
Woodgate. *W Sus* 2B **44**
Wood Green. *G Lon* 2A **18**
Woodham. *Surr* 2C **25**
Woodham Ferrers. *Essx* 2B **20**
Woodham Mortimer. *Essx* 1C **21**
Woodham Walter. *Essx* 1C **21**
Woodingdean. *Brig* 2B **46**
Woodlands. *Kent* 2D **27**
Woodlands Park. *Wind* 1A **24**
Woodley. *Wok* 1D **23**
Woodmancote. *W Sus* 2D **43**
  (nr. Chichester)
Woodmancote. *W Sus* 1A **46**
  (nr. Henfield)
Woodmancott. *Hants* 1B **32**
Woodmansgreen. *W Sus* 3A **34**
Woodmansterne. *Surr* 3A **26**
Woodnesborough. *Kent* 3D **31**
Wood's Green. *E Sus* 2A **38**
Woodside. *Brac* 1B **24**
Woodside. *Herts* 1A **18**
Woodstock. *Oxon* 3A **4**
Wood Street Village. *Surr* 3B **24**
Woolage Green. *Kent* 1C **41**
Woolage Village. *Kent* 3C **31**
Woolbeding. *W Sus* 3A **34**

Woolhampton. *W Ber* 2B **22**
Woolmer Green. *Herts* 3A **8**
Woolston. *Sotn* 1A **42**
Woolton Hill. *Hants* 2A **22**
Woolverstone. *Suff* 1B **12**
Woolwich. *G Lon* 1C **27**
Wootton. *IOW* 3B **42**
Wootton. *Kent* 1C **41**
Wootton. *Oxon* 1A **14**
  (nr. Abingdon)
Wootton. *Oxon* 3A **4**
  (nr. Woodstock)
Wootton Bridge. *IOW* 3B **42**
Wootton Common. *IOW* 3B **42**
Wootton St Lawrence. *Hants* 3B **22**
Worcester Park. *G Lon* 2A **26**
Workhouse Green. *Suff* 1D **11**
Worlds End. *Hants* 1C **43**
World's End. *W Ber* 1A **22**
World's End. *W Sus* 1B **46**
Wormingford. *Essx* 1D **11**
Worminghall. *Buck* 1C **15**
Wormley. *Herts* 1B **18**
Wormley. *Surr* 2B **34**
Wormshill. *Kent* 3C **29**
Worplesdon. *Surr* 3B **24**
Worth. *Kent* 3D **31**
Worth. *W Sus* 2B **36**
Worthing. *W Sus* 2D **45**
Worting. *Hants* 3C **23**
Wotton. *Surr* 1D **35**
Wotton Underwood. *Buck* 3C **5**
Wouldham. *Kent* 2B **28**
Wrabness. *Essx* 1B **12**
Wraysbury. *Wind* 1C **25**
Wrecclesham. *Surr* 1A **34**
Wright's Green. *Essx* 3D **9**
Writtle. *Essx* 1A **20**
Wrotham. *Kent* 3A **28**
Wrotham Heath. *Kent* 3A **28**
Wroxton. *Oxon* 1A **4**
Wyatt's Green. *Essx* 2D **19**
Wych Cross. *E Sus* 2C **37**
Wyck. *Hants* 2D **33**
Wycombe Marsh. *Buck* 2A **16**
Wyddial. *Herts* 1B **8**
Wye. *Kent* 1A **40**
Wyfold Grange. *Oxon* 3C **15**
Wyke. *Surr* 3B **24**
Wymering. *Port* 2C **43**
Wytham. *Oxon* 1A **14**

Y

Yalding. *Kent* 3A **28**
Yapton. *W Sus* 2B **44**
Yarmouth. *IOW* 3A **42**
Yarnton. *Oxon* 3A **4**
Yateley. *Hants* 2A **24**
Yattendon. *W Ber* 1B **22**
Yeading. *G Lon* 3D **17**
Yelford. *Oxon* 1A **14**
Yelsted. *Kent* 2C **29**
Yiewsley. *G Lon* 3C **17**
Yorkletts. *Kent* 2A **30**
Young's End. *Essx* 3B **10**

The representation on the maps of a road, track or footpath is no evidence of the existence of a right of way.

The Grid on this atlas is the National Grid taken from Ordnance Survey mapping with the permission of the Controller of Her Majesty's Stationery Office.

CITY & TOWN CENTRE PLANS

Reference to Town Plans

MOTORWAY	**M2**	TOLL	HOSPITAL	H
MOTORWAY UNDER CONSTRUCTION		RAILWAY AND STATION	INFORMATION CENTRE	ℹ
MOTORWAY PROPOSED		UNDERGROUND/METRO & DLR STATION	DLR	LIGHTHOUSE
MOTORWAY JUNCTIONS WITH NUMBERS		LEVEL CROSSING AND TUNNEL	MARKET
Unlimited Interchange **4**		TRAM STOP AND ONE WAY TRAM STOP	NATIONAL TRUST PROPERTY (Open) NT
Limited Interchange **5**		BUILT-UP AREA	(Restricted opening) NT
PRIMARY ROUTE	**A21**	ABBEY, CATHEDRAL, PRIORY ETC. †	PARK & RIDE
DUAL CARRIAGEWAYS	**A260**	AIRPORT ✈	PLACE OF INTEREST
CLASS A ROAD		BUS STATION	POLICE STATION ▲
CLASS B ROAD	**B2011**	CAR PARK (Selection of) P	POST OFFICE ★
MAJOR ROADS UNDER CONSTRUCTION		CHURCH †	SHOPPING AREA
MAJOR ROADS PROPOSED		CITY WALL	(Main street and precinct)
MINOR ROADS		FERRY (Vehicular)	SHOPMOBILITY
RESTRICTED ACCESS		(Foot only)	TOILET
PEDESTRIAN ROAD & MAIN FOOTWAY		GOLF COURSE	VIEWPOINT
ONE WAY STREETS		HELIPORT	

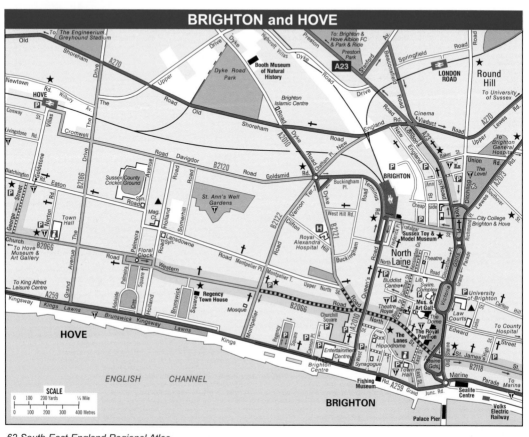

BRIGHTON and HOVE

SCALE
0 100 200 Yards ¼ Mile
0 100 200 300 400 Metres

ENGLISH CHANNEL

HOVE

BRIGHTON

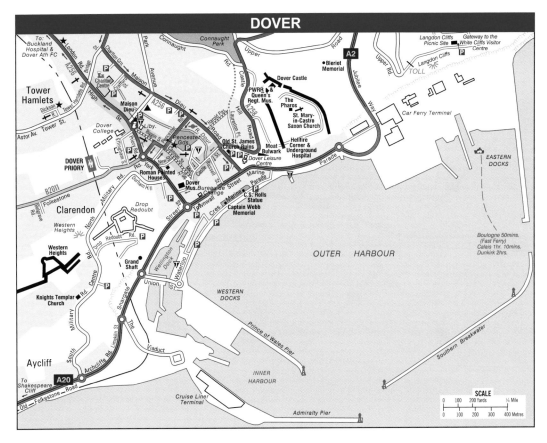

DOVER

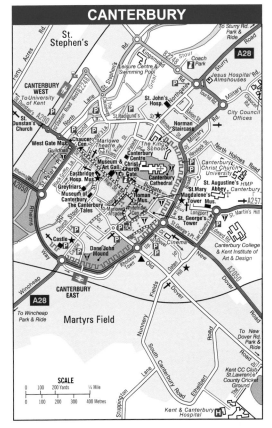

CANTERBURY

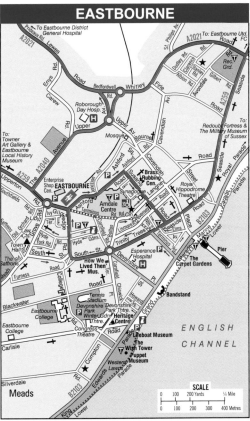

EASTBOURNE

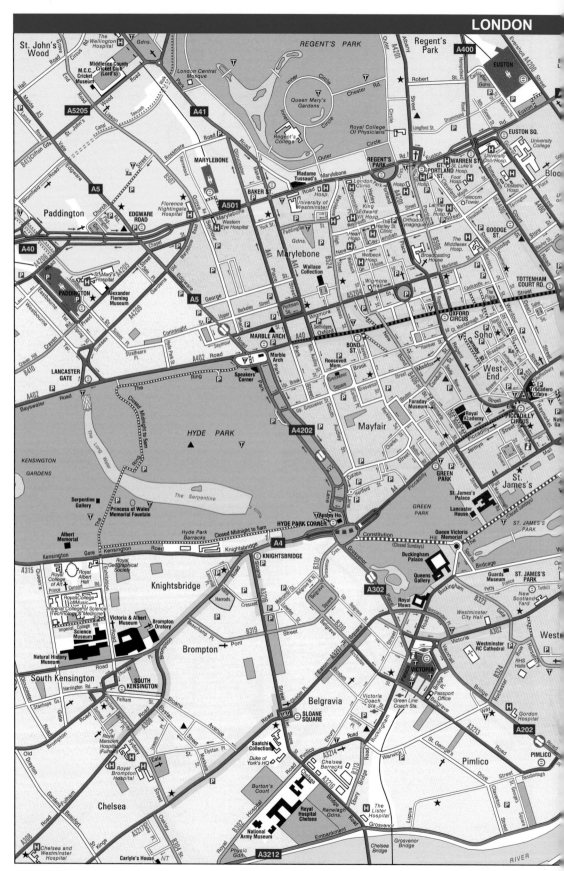

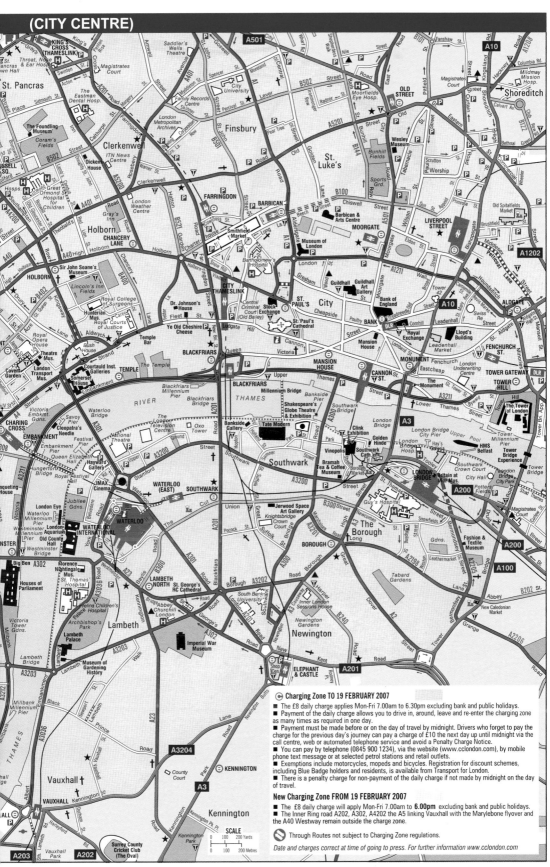

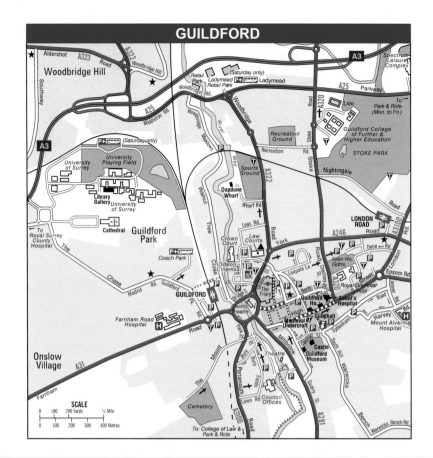

GUILDFORD

Aldershot · A323 · Road · A322

Woodbridge Hill

Woodbridge Hill

Spectrum Leisure Complex

A3

A25 · Parkway

(Saturday only)

Retail Park · Ladymead Retail Park · P+ Ladymead

Middleton Rd.

A25

Woodbridge · Rd.

Woodbridge Rd.

River Wey

Southway

Lido

To Park & Ride (Mon. to Fri.)

Stoke · A320

Road

Stoke

Guildford College of Further & Higher Education

Recreation Ground

Recreation · Rd.

STOKE PARK

A3

P+ (Saturday only)

University of Surrey

University Playing Field

Library Gallery · University of Surrey

Cathedral

Guildford Park

Meadows

Walnut Tree Close

Sports Ground

Dapdune Wharf

Wharf Rd.

Leas Rd.

Nightingale

A322

To Royal Surrey County Hospital

The Chase

Madrid · Rd. · Guildford

Coach Park · P+

Crown Court

Law Courts

Odeon Cinema

York · Road

LONDON ROAD

A246

Allen Ho. Gdns.

Dene · Rd.

London Rd.

Epsom Rd.

A3100

Leapale La.

North St.

Royal Grammar School

Harvey · Rd.

Rinner Rd.

Farnham Road Hospital · H

GUILDFORD

Electric Theatre

The Friary

Guildford Ho.

Lib.

Abbot's Hospital

High · St.

Sydenham · Rd.

Mount Alvernia Hospital

Onslow Village

A31

Medieval Undercroft

Guildhall

Guildford Museum

Castle

Sydenham Rd.

Castle · Hill

Warwicks

Bench · Rd.

Farnham · Road

Mount · St.

Portsmouth · Road

Fields

Theatre

Quarry · St.

Millbrook

A3100

A281

Lawn · Rd.

Council Offices

Cemetery

To: College of Law & Park & Ride

SCALE

0 100 200 Yards ¼ Mile

0 100 200 300 400 Metres

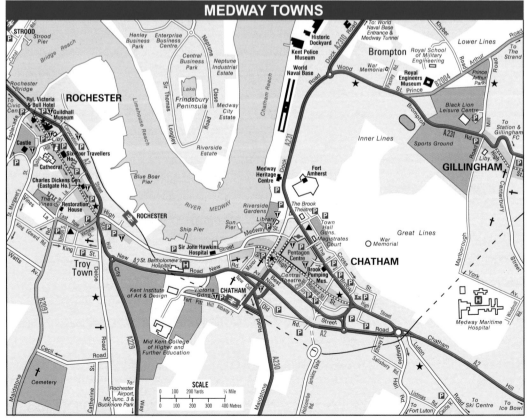

MEDWAY TOWNS

STROOD

Strood Pier

Canal

Bridge · Reach

Henley Business Park

Enterprise Business Centre

Central Business Park

Neptune Industrial Estate

Neptune · Close

To: World Naval Base Entrance & Medway Tunnel

Historic Dockyard

Kent Police Museum

World Naval Base

Dock · A2310 · Road

Wood · Road

Brompton

Royal School of Military Engineering

War Memorial

Royal Engineers Museum

St. · Prince

Lower Lines

To The Strand

B2004

Prince Arthur Park

Khyber · Road

Arthur

Rochester Bridge

Rochester Castle

Ryl. Victoria & Bull Hotel

ROCHESTER

Guildhall Museum

Castle

Liby.

Six Poor Travellers Ho.

Cathedral

Charles Dickens Cen. (Eastgate Ho.)

The Vines

Restoration House

Sir Thomas Longley Rd.

Lake

Frindsbury Peninsula

Limehouse · Reach

Medway City Estate

Riverside Estate

Blue Boar Pier

Chatham · Reach

A231 · Dock · Road

Inner Lines

Sports Ground

A231 · Rd.

Black Lion Leisure Centre

To Station & Gillingham FC

Liby.

GILLINGHAM

Canterbury · St.

St. Margaret's · St.

King Edward Rd.

Watts · Av.

Vines · La.

East · Row

High · St.

King · St.

ROCHESTER

Ship Pier

RIVER · MEDWAY

Sun Pier

Medway

Medway Heritage Centre

Fort Amherst

Riverside Gardens

The Brook Theatre

Library

Town Hall Gdns.

Magistrates Court

Great · Lines

War Memorial

Marlborough · Road

York · Street

Troy Town

B2097

Delce

A2 · St. Bartholomew's Hospital · H

Sir John Hawkins Hospital

New · Road

New · Rd.

New · Cut

Manor · Rd.

Pentagon Centre

Central Theatre

Brook Pumping Mus.

High · St.

Cross · St.

CHATHAM

Street

Kent Institute of Art & Design

Victoria Gdns.

CHATHAM

Fort · Pitt · Hill

Albany · T.

Old · Rd.

High · Street

Maidstone

A229

Cecil · Road

Mid Kent College of Higher and Further Education

A230

Maidstone · Way

Jenkins · Dale

Holcombe · Road

A2

Salisbury · Rd.

Magpie · Hall · Road

Chatham

Luton

Cemetery

Catherine · Street

To: Rochester Airport, M2 Junc. 3 & Buckmore Park

Windmill · Rd.

Medway Maritime Hospital

Listmas · Rd.

To Ski Centre

To Ice Bowl

To Fort Luton

SCALE

0 100 200 Yards ¼ Mile

0 100 200 300 400 Metres

66 South East England Regional Atlas

MILTON KEYNES

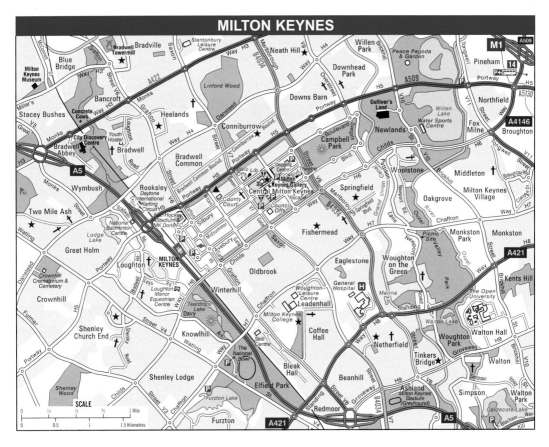

OXFORD

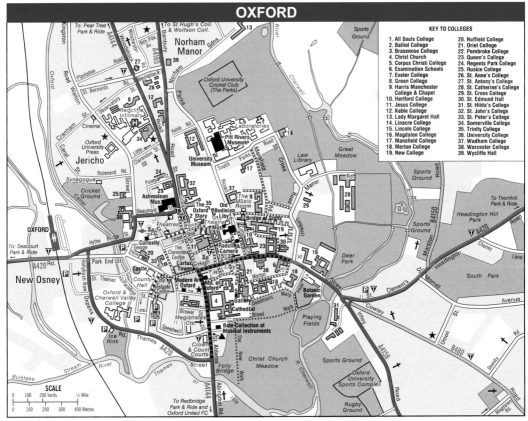

KEY TO COLLEGES

1. All Souls College
2. Balliol College
3. Brasenose College
4. Christ Church
5. Corpus Christi College
6. Examination Schools
7. Exeter College
8. Green College
9. Harris Manchester College & Chapel
10. Hertford College
11. Jesus College
12. Keble College
13. Lady Margaret Hall
14. Linacre College
15. Lincoln College
16. Magdalen College
17. Mansfield College
18. Merton College
19. New College
20. Nuffield College
21. Oriel College
22. Pembroke College
23. Queen's College
24. Regents Park College
25. Ruskin College
26. St. Anne's College
27. St. Antony's College
28. St. Catherine's College
29. St. Cross College
30. St. Edmund Hall
31. St. Hilda's College
32. St. John's College
33. St. Peter's College
34. Somerville College
35. Trinity College
36. University College
37. Wadham College
38. Worcester College
39. Wycliffe Hall

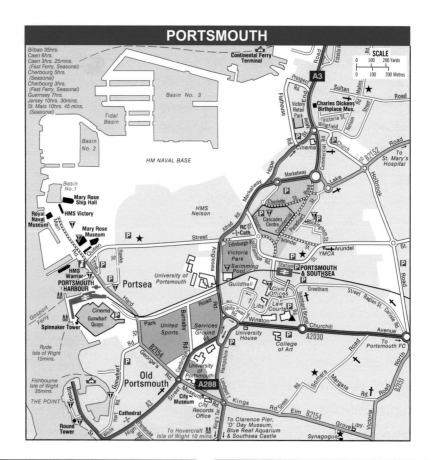

PORTSMOUTH

Bilbao 35hrs.
Caen 6hrs.
Caen 3hrs. 25mins.
(Fast Ferry, Seasonal)
Cherbourg 5hrs.
(Seasonal)
Cherbourg 3hrs.
(Fast Ferry, Seasonal)
Jersey 10hrs. 30mins.
St. Malo 10hrs. 45 mins.
(Seasonal)

Continental Ferry Terminal

SCALE
0   100   200 Yards
0   100   200 Metres

Basin No. 3

Tidal Basin

Basin No. 2

HM NAVAL BASE

Basin No.1

Charles Dickens Birthplace Mus.

Mary Rose Ship Hall
HMS Victory
Royal Naval Museum
Mary Rose Museum

HMS Nelson

Cascades Centre

RC Cath.

HMS Warrior
PORTSMOUTH HARBOUR

Portsea

University of Portsmouth

Victoria Park
Swimming Pool

Guildhall

Civic Offices

PORTSMOUTH & SOUTHSEA

Law Courts

Gosport Ferry

Cinema
Gunwharf Quays

Spinnaker Tower

Ryde Isle of Wight 15mins.

Park

United Sports

Services Ground

University House

College of Art

To Portsmouth FC

Fishbourne Isle of Wight 35mins.

THE POINT

Old Portsmouth

University of Portsmouth

Street Museum
City Museum

City Records Office

Cathedral

Round Tower

To Clarence Pier, 'D' Day Museum, Blue Reef Aquarium & Southsea Castle

To Hovercraft Isle of Wight 10 mins.

Synagogue

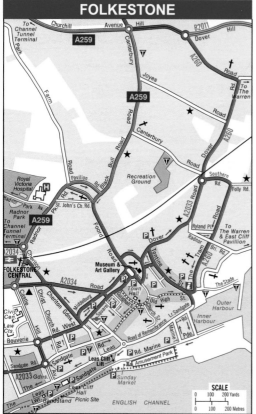

FOLKESTONE

To Channel Tunnel Terminal

Churchill   Avenue   Hill

A259

B2011

Dover Hill

To The Warren

Royal Victoria Hospital

Radnor Park

To Channel Tunnel Terminal

A259

A2034

FOLKESTONE CENTRAL

Recreation Ground

Museum & Art Gallery

Town Hall

Old High St.

To The Warren & East Cliff Pavillion

Outer Harbour

Inner Harbour

Civic Cen.

Law Cts.

Bouverie

Road of Remembrance

Leas Cliff Lift

Amusement Park

Sandgate Rd.

Sunday Market

Leas Cliff Hall

Bandstand

Picnic Site

SCALE
0   100   200 Yards
0   100   200 Metres

ENGLISH CHANNEL

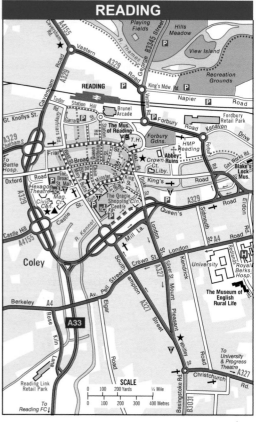

READING

A4155

Playing Fields

Hills Meadow

View Island

Recreation Grounds

Vastern

A329

READING

Brunel Arcade

King's Mdw. Rd.

Napier   Road

Fordbury Retail Park

Station Hill

The Mus. of Reading

Forbury Gdns.

HMP Reading

Gt. Knollys St.

Tudor

Friar

Abbey Ruins

Blake's Lock Mus.

To Battle Hosp.

Broad

Crown

Oxford

Hexagon Theatre

St. Mall

King's   Road

Civic Cr.

The Oracle Shopping Ctr. Centre

Queen's

Castle Hill

R. Kennet

A4155

Coley

Castle

University

Royal Berks. Hosp.

Berkeley   A4

The Museum of English Rural Life

A33

To University & Progress Theatre

Reading Link Retail Park

SCALE
0   100   200 Yards
0   100   200   300   400 Metres

¼ Mile

To Reading FC

Christchurch   A327

B3031

68 South East England Regional Atlas

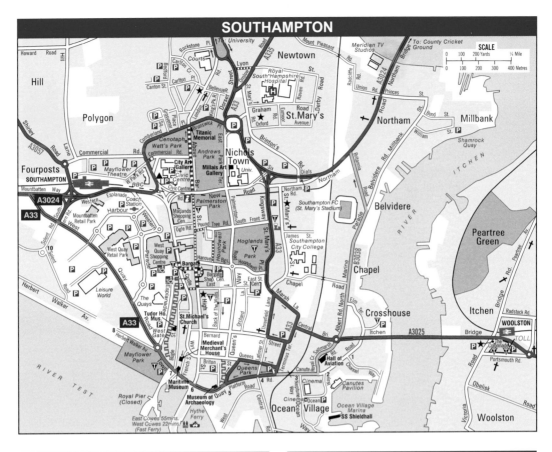

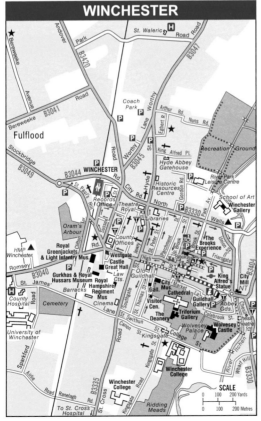

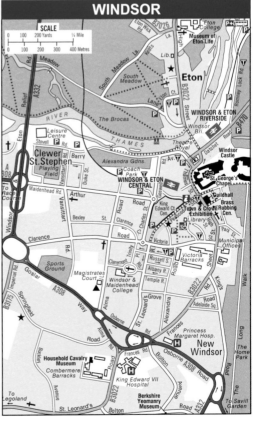

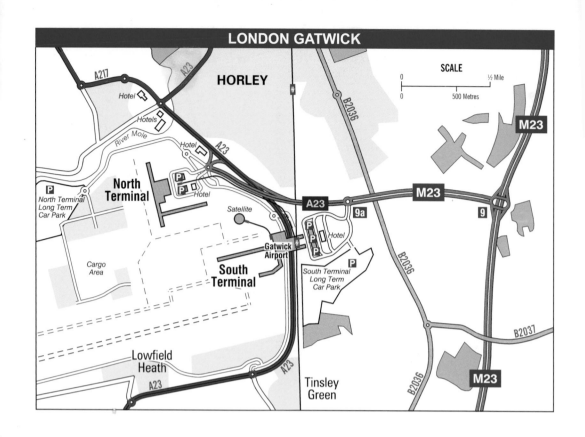

LONDON GATWICK

HORLEY

SCALE

North Terminal

Satellite

Gatwick Airport

South Terminal

Cargo Area

North Terminal Long Term Car Park

South Terminal Long Term Car Park

Lowfield Heath

Tinsley Green

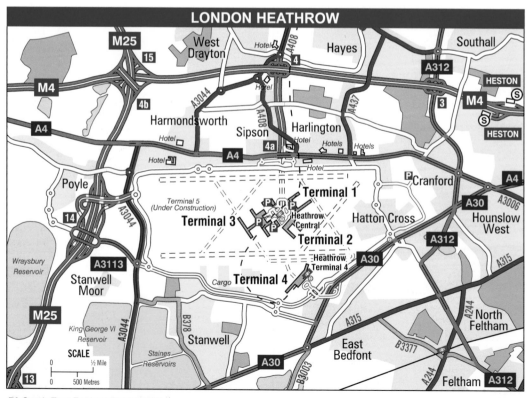

LONDON HEATHROW

West Drayton

Hayes

Southall

HESTON

HESTON

Harmondsworth

Sipson

Harlington

Cranford

Poyle

Terminal 5 (Under Construction)

Terminal 3

Terminal 1

Heathrow Central

Hatton Cross

Hounslow West

Terminal 2

Wraysbury Reservoir

Stanwell Moor

Heathrow Terminal 4

Cargo

Terminal 4

North Feltham

King George VI Reservoir

Stanwell

East Bedfont

Staines Reservoirs

Feltham

SCALE

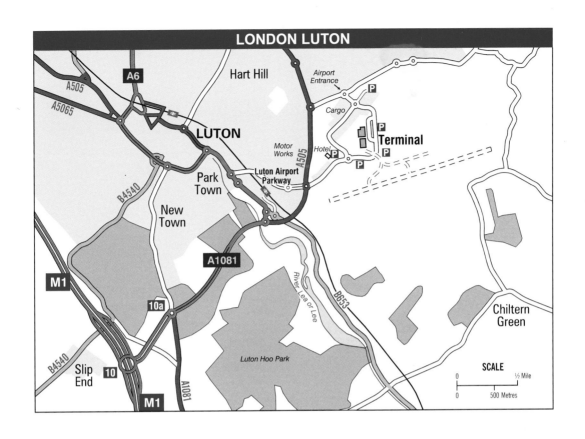

LONDON LUTON

A6 · A505 · A5065 · Hart Hill · Airport Entrance · **LUTON** · Cargo · P · P · Motor Works · Hotel · P · P · **Terminal** · P · A505 · Luton Airport Parkway · Park Town · New Town · B4540 · A1081 · M1 · 10a · River Lea or Lee · B653 · Chiltern Green · B4540 · Slip End · 10 · A1081 · M1 · Luton Hoo Park

SCALE
0 — ½ Mile
0 — 500 Metres

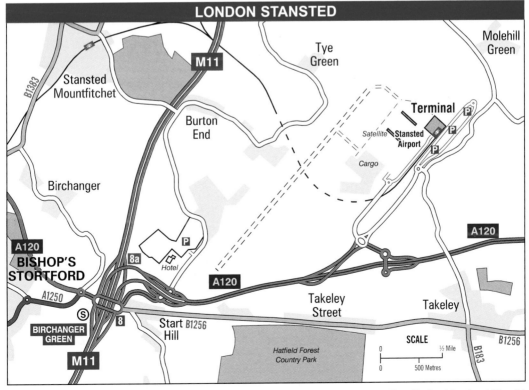

LONDON STANSTED

B1383 · Stansted Mountfitchet · M11 · Tye Green · Molehill Green · **Terminal** · P · P · Satellite · **Stansted Airport** · P · Burton End · Cargo · Birchanger · A120 · A120 · **BISHOP'S STORTFORD** · 8a · P · Hotel · A120 · A1250 · S · **BIRCHANGER GREEN** · 8 · Start Hill · B1256 · Takeley Street · Takeley · B1256 · M11 · B183 · Hatfield Forest Country Park

SCALE
0 — ½ Mile
0 — 500 Metres

South East England Regional Atlas 71

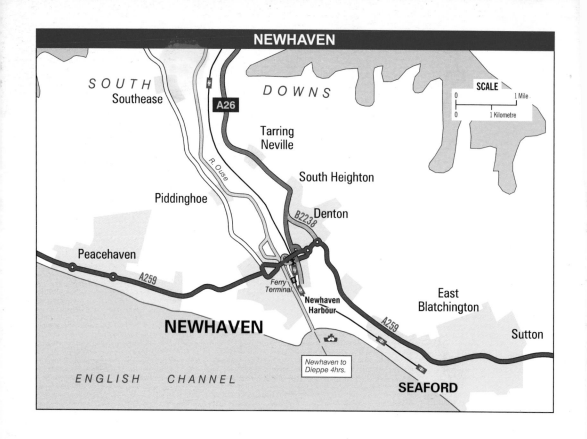

NEWHAVEN

SOUTH

Southease

DOWNS

A26

Tarring
Neville

South Heighton

B2238

Denton

Piddinghoe

R. Ouse

Peacehaven

A259

Ferry
Terminal

Newhaven
Harbour

East
Blatchington

Sutton

NEWHAVEN

A259

ENGLISH CHANNEL

Newhaven to
Dieppe 4hrs.

SEAFORD

SCALE
0   1 Mile
0   1 Kilometre

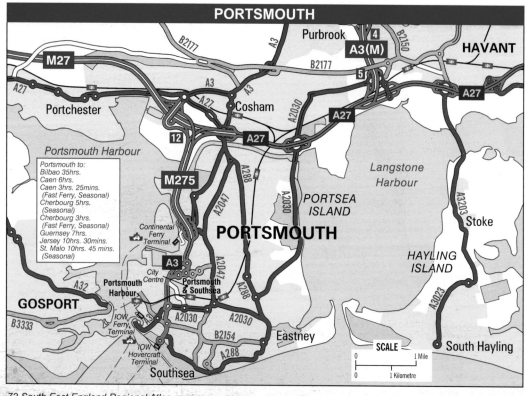

PORTSMOUTH

B2177

A3

Purbrook

4

A3(M)

B2150

HAVANT

M27

B2177

5

A27

A27

A3

A3

A27

Portchester

A27

A27

Cosham

A2030

A2030

12

A27

Portsmouth Harbour

Portsmouth to:
Bilbao 35hrs.
Caen 6hrs.
Caen 3hrs. 25mins.
(Fast Ferry, Seasonal)
Cherbourg 5hrs.
(Seasonal)
Cherbourg 3hrs.
(Fast Ferry, Seasonal)
Guernsey 7hrs.
Jersey 10hrs. 30mins.
St. Malo 10hrs. 45 mins.
(Seasonal)

M275

A288

Langstone
Harbour

A2030

A3203

Stoke

*PORTSEA
ISLAND*

A2047

Continental
Ferry
Terminal

PORTSMOUTH

*HAYLING
ISLAND*

A3

City
Centre

A2047

A288

A3023

GOSPORT

A32

**Portsmouth
Harbour**

**Portsmouth
& Southsea**

B3333

IOW
Ferry
Terminal

A2030

A2030

A288

IOW
Hovercraft
Terminal

A2030

B2154

Eastney

South Hayling

Southsea

SCALE
0   1 Mile
0   1 Kilometre